Donna F. Orchard

Behind the Schoolhouse Door

BOOK III OF ROUGHNECK SERIES

HISTORICAL FICTION

PORTLAND • OREGON
INKWATERPRESS.COM

Other books by Donna F. Orchard:

The Roughneck Series:

Roughneck Daddy: A Memoir
Book I

Roughneck: A Daughter's Story
Book II

For Marilyn

Contents

ACKNOWLEDGEMENTS

Thank you Dr. Ed White for your interest in my career when I arrived in Mobile, a newcomer in need of a mentor.

Marilyn Sewell, my sister, has given me practical tools for writing over the years and the inspiration to use them.

Thank you, Jim Fulmer, for being a faithful, loving brother.

May Laughton was the first person to see Schoolhouse in its infancy. Thank you for the editing help early on and the fun we had laughing at the lines that did not make the cut.

There would not be a book without the thousands of schoolchildren over the years who pushed me full into life.

I am thankful always for my two boys, Al and Benjamin, who give me great joy, and now my grandchildren: Clara, Wells, Ella, and Mack.

I could not be productive without the Al-Anon program and the special moments with my Al- Anon friends in and out of meetings.

My partner, Bill, stepped up and did much of the editing on this book. Thank you for your patience and enthusiastic support of my work in many different ways.

Donna center
Putting her best foot forward at Renville High

Today it (education) is a principal instrument in awakening the child to cultural values, in preparing him for later professional training, and in helping him to adjust normally to his environment. In these days, it is doubtful that any child may reasonably be expected to succeed in life if he is denied the opportunity of an education. Such an opportunity, where the state has undertaken to provide it, is a right which must be made available to all on equal terms.

BROWN V BOARD OF EDUCATION OF TOPEKA 1954

Chapter 1
THIS IS MY CASTLE

6:45 a.m.
Renville High School

Though heat still rose from the sidewalk in September, I was exuberant when rounding the path to circular stone steps leading to the handsome 1950s red brick schoolhouse. Three stories with long windows were framed by white columns, stout shoulders to hoist public schools and John Dewey and democracy; then, the safety of a twelve foot door of dark brown planks and iron latch, my castle.

It was the first minute of my first job: girls' physical education teacher and basketball coach at Renville High School. The small town in North Louisiana was not far from where I grew up.

Ignoring the stares and a wolf whistle that went unchecked, I nudged my way through the crowd of students, tall basketball player types pressed against the entrance.

I urged the massive door open and walked inside to a strong smell of ink. Teachers were dancing around the swishing and whirling of the purple drum to catch flying mimeograph pages. *All Visitors Sign in at the Office.*

How could I know what was to come: secrets—unacknowledged, oblique, some real, some mythical—that lay inside these walls after the doors were shut behind me? My father used to say of his life on an oil rig, "It's a different world, baby, a different world." Stepping inside those doors in 1969, it would be forty years before I realized how inured I became to keeping the secrets in my world of public education— the good and the not so good.

Secret number one: I got this job right out of school because the superintendent of schools recognized my last name. My uncle was a dean in the education department at LSU.

I turned twenty-two one month before. When I looked up at the man-sized students at the door, I could no longer keep the secret to myself—high schoolers were not yet adults, but close to it—some seventeen, eighteen, even nineteen years old.

No one noticed me as I stood around; arms crossed balancing on one foot and then the other. I thought Principle Ingleside would be in the hall to greet me with his preacher hair that never moved. He smiled when there was nothing to smile about. In the interview, he grinned through the whole story of the former P.E. teacher's cancer treatment.

I knew he was there. Mr. Ingleside reminded me several times during my interview of the importance of being punctual. He greeted the students as they jumped off the steps of the yellow school bus each morning to chat with the driver. The bus driver, ostensibly an auxiliary hand, was the first person to see the students in the morning and the last person to wave good-bye to them in the afternoon. They often flushed out any problems brought to school from the neighborhoods and alerted the principal.

This was not what I expected. I had no idea where the gym was so I gawked through the glass. As I processed this launch of the school day: *Why are these teachers not cackling carefree, smiling and laughing on the first day of school? Shoulders are pulled up tense, wrinkled brows, furtive whispers.* My grandmother might have said, "Looks like everybody's on pins and needles."

The teachers' boxes faced me as I walked into the office: Mrs. Donna Orchard, class rolls and a grade book. *Somebody knows I'm here.*

The disinterested chairs that lined the wall, like the setup for a junior high dance, added to the chill. These chairs would not be empty again until the end of the year, chairs no one wanted to sit in—students, teachers or parents. Each person would assume the same status in anticipation of the call to 'step in' through the fancy glass door with leaded inlay: Principal.

The door was closed. I wandered back out into the hall.

Suddenly, breaking the monotonous rhythm, the metal latch behind me banged and both sides of the tall doors opened to a wave of heat on my neck. The machines stopped. Speech stopped. Down the hall were dark hollow eyes dotting up and down, side to side in the stillness of a pointillism painting, all tending the door. I turned and squinted though the morning sun. In the doorway were three figures in the haze, stiff-necked white men in black suits, matching white shirts, and skinny black ties—a standoff at the end of a dusty street in an old western movie. They moved in quickly.

One of the men turned around… looked me in the eye, "No students allowed on this hall before the bell," he said.

"But sir, I'm a teacher."

"Sorry, little lady."

They fanned out and disappeared.

Someone caught my elbow, "Federal Marshals." *Oh. Oh no. Little Rock, Arkansas, 1957*; the media images of paratroopers falling from the sky with bayonets became players in this backdrop of my present drama.

Are they here to enforce the 1954 Brown v the Board? Is this possible? I thought segregation was safely in the past.

Every school in the South had a desegregation plan in place by 1964.

Even my segregated high school in Del City, my hometown, had started the integration process in 1966, the year after I left.

This was 1969.

My mind went to the backlog of times I had stood haplessly looking down a long hall. *I don't belong here*—Carroll High School. During my teacher training, I was assigned an observation in this large all-black high school in Monroe. The apprehension in the school that day was palpable. Soon their building would be picked up, shaken up, mixed up, *for their own good.* Mine was the only white face in the school that day my first experience being a minority. I was not prepared for my awkwardness or my overwhelming flight response. None of the handsome black women dressed in suits and silk blouses spoke when I walked in, a young student in their teacher's lounge. Now I understand why.

The Ryland Parish School System in Renville must have figured it would take the government a while to get around to desegregating all the small schools in North Louisiana. They took their own sweet time to comply. *Now look who are here, the Marshals!* Why didn't the principal warn me? All he talked about in my interview was knowing my Uncle Lemos at LSU.

"This is a fine damn how do you do" is what my daddy said when I told him about my first assignment, a man not given to nuance. I was a first year teacher, not much older than my students, on three years' probation—when I could get fired for no reason—and now I found myself in this hot spot, trying to fly under the radar screen and duck G-men, and not the ones from an old FBI movie.

The bell rang and the flood of students burst through the door past me. Clumps of kids were divided, black and white loudly neighboring—all eyes on me. I was in their space and they knew it. They seemed comfortable enough with what would certainly be a milestone, but even if they were not, they had their buddies. I was alone in the only nice dress I owned, this bright green shift.

The gym should have a double door and big locks. There it was. *At least I've found my first class*. There must have been 100 students just milling around in the gym. I heard a whistle but nobody was paying attention. *I don't have a whistle. What can I do?*

I wrote my name in big letters and climbed up to the top of the bleachers.

The man in grey stretch Bermuda shorts stopped blowing his whistle and walked toward me, "What ya doing way up there on the bleachers?"

"I'm holding up a sign to try to find my class."

"Well, that's easy. You have all the girls this period and I have the boys," he said with smiling eyes.

"You the new P.E. teacher? I'm Terry." He waved his arm, "You can have this part of the bleachers by the girls' dressing room. I'll be down here. Don't let 'em go in the back for any reason. They'll be back there smoking. You got a roll? Just call the roll. They'll come when they hear their name."

As he turned around, I got a whiff of something, Aqua Velva. Daddy splashed it on after a shave.

Too bad the coach didn't have time for a shave. Gee, it was the first day of school. He could be good looking, a football type with a big neck, broad shoulders, and a nice butt.

"Okay, Terry. I'm Mrs. Orchard, Donna."

I need some Aqua Velva myself. Sweat is dripping down my nylons.

The plan at Renville High was that the black high school students moved into the white high school. All middle schoolers moved into the building across town in the African- American neighborhood. It all happened that day.

I expected an assembly program to welcome the new students and teachers, something. The principal should have opened school to organize the routine—looked us in the eye—given us his vision.

I motioned and shouted, "All girls sit on the bleachers over here."

"Ma'am," a tiny girl said, "I need to go to the bathroom. I'm ninth grade. I don't know where to go."

"Huh? Just a minute."

"I got to go bad."

"Well, go on in the back to the dressing room, but hurry."

I'm already breaking a rule. I heard that gray noise like ocean waves crashing in my ears, a signal that I was losing it.

"Girls, if you have 'Fulmer'—oh, I just got married—I mean 'Orchard' on your schedule for homeroom and first period, take a seat on the bleachers. If you don't, another teacher is looking for you." Many of the girls had bows in their hair and their white blouses with Peter Pan collars were as crisp and sparking as their faces—the first day of school.

"Line up in front of me with your schedules and I'll send you where you need to go. We have to get an exact count today, a perfect count."

"I'm supposed to have history first period, but I want to get that changed to P.E.," a student poked her schedule in my face.

"That's Kelly. Mrs. Kelly is your first period teacher. Take off to B-3."

"Where's it at?"

"Well, I'm not sure. Ask somebody in the hall."

Long legs in black fishnet nylons pushed through the first three rows of girls on the front bleachers—to bound onto the floor, heading out, "I'll take her! I'll take her!"

These kids can't run all over the building.

"No, you come back here. Turn right around where you are and we'll talk about those hose later."

"Who's that dressed up man peeking in the door?" she said, as she followed my directions and came back to sit down. "He's staring at you."

"Who knows? Just ignore it." *At this point I don't care if God himself observes me.*

"Now is everybody in the right place?"

When I looked up from the roll, I saw that all the black students were sitting on one side of the bleachers and the white students on the other. *Mr. FBI man will not like that. I will fix it tomorrow. They will be in their squad lines in alphabetical order.*

Stumbling over their names on the first day will not be good.

"Cathy Armand"

"Here"

"Maddy Arnold"

"Here"

"Latrisha Arrendale"

"That's Treeeesha."

"Sorry."

"Gay Nell Lane, do you go by Gay or Nell?"

"Will you give me a basketball Miss Lady? This class is boring."

"What's your name?" I looked up to the back row at the small African-American student.

"Asia." she said.

"I am Mrs. Orchard. I have asked you to raise your hand if you have a question."

Asia's hand went up.

"We play basketball days we don't dress out and my grandmaw says she can't afford to buy a new gym suit. I'll have to wear my red one right on."

"This is still homeroom."

I glanced down at the floor and saw my note from the principal that was taped to the roll. "Give the office an accurate black and white count. This is very important. If someone comes in late anytime during the day, add them."

I had no idea who was black or white. I did not look up when they answered. *How could I be so stupid to forget that? How am I going to do this? I'll make up something.*

"Girls, when I call your name, raise your hand. I want to put your name with your face."

"This lady's crazy. She's calling the roll twice. Are P.E. teachers real teachers? Did you have to go to school for that?"

Asia sure is a little girl to have such a big mouth.

"Mrs. Orchard," yelled Coach Terry from the other end of the gym, "Send me Cindy Crane."

"Pardon?"

"I need her to call my roll. She's my assistant first period. She'll be with me every day. I'll keep her on my roll and give her a grade each quarter."

"Ah…okay. Cindy you can go."

"Class, now I'm going to read over the syllabus."

"The what?"

"It's the schedule of activities for the semester. We'll start with tennis."

"Tennis!" I heard groans, then a snippety reply, "This's sure gonna be a boring class," Asia again.

"This white lady don't know nothin' 'bout basketball. I hear she's the coach," Latrisha said.

"All right, settle down. I asked you to raise your hand if you have a question." I saw a hand. "What's your name?"

"Thought you were gonna remember my name. It's Asia."

"Of course." *How could I forget?*

"What we doin' over here anyway? What was your name, Miss Lady?"

"Thought you were going to remember my name, Asia. It is Mrs. Orchard, just like the apple orchard." *At least I got a laugh out of them.*

"What we doin'over here anyway, 'Mis..sus' Orchard? It stinks up here on these bleachers. Smells like pole cat."

The blond girl with a ponytail squirmed around from the front row to look at Asia. She'd had enough. "Well, we don't want you over here either! And my mama's sure not buying a new gym uniform. We've always had gold or green for the Hornets."

"Girls, settle down. I will not have you shouting. Raise your hand to speak. These are the rules. They will be typed up tomorrow."

I'm jangled in all this racket. No, this is blind panic.

I turned away while I tried to breathe—*breathe in deep; let it out slowly, ten counts.*

How do I explain 100 years of slavery and bad feelings while I call the roll? Can a Supreme Court ruling outlaw perceptions, bias, and prejudice? Looks like I am about to find out.

There's the bell. "It will be all right, girls..." I looked up to the ceiling in reflection. "We'll get through these changes together."

When I looked down, I was talking to empty bleachers.

Today, education is perhaps the most important function of state and local governments. Compulsory school attendance laws and the great expenditures for education both demonstrate our recognition of the importance of education to our democratic society. It is required in the performance of our most basic public responsibilities, even service in the armed forces. It is the very foundation of good citizenship.

BROWN V. BOARD OF EDUCATION OF TOPEKA 1954.

Chapter 2

REALITY AT RENVILLE

Finally silence. It was 2:45 p.m. and the end of my first day. I said the same thing for five periods. If Asia was still here, I'd tell her, "You're right, my class was boring!" Tomorrow I must ease off; get quiet when I have a break.

What's that smell? My hand went over my nose as I headed for my office in the back. There it was, mildew from the sweaty socks and shirts spilling out of lockers, lying on benches; probably there all summer. I have a lot of clean up to do.

I flopped papers down on the workspace then paused to give the top of the desk a second look, extraordinary old wood. Country pine. I stroked the honey colored grain. *It is really quite good*. Let's see, this was a style at the end of the 1930s. My finger traced each deep gash as I wondered how many other teachers and coaches had employed it. Who circled sweating teams around the old desk at halftime? What did a disappointed coach say to revive her team, to turn the momentum around to ultimately win the game? This handsome piece had heard it all. *Maybe I'll restore it.*

My swivel chair was oak, definitely from the 30s. There was a sweet little cushion, blue and red flowers at my back, a nice touch. I cannot believe they left something. This place was stripped. There was no tape dispenser, no scissors. Somebody had tape in here. The wall was speckled with old yellow strips, a height and weight chart dangling sideways.

Teachers take everything when they leave. They need their supplies at the next school. The thirty-five dollar supplement for materials did not go far. I found out quickly that dipping into my own pocket at the beginning of the year would be commonplace.

In the middle desk drawer was a sandwich bag with a few dollars and some change, probably from selling gym suits or from a fundraiser. Somebody in the office will know. I felt a key in the very back. I hope it fits that supply closet. Maybe there's some good stuff inside. It worked! My luck had to change today. Let's see what I can use... Yeah, a new chart. We will get to know each other during the assessments. Here's a poster with the five food groups. Wonder where those heavy, buttery cafeteria rolls fit in? They are in a class of their own. Yum.

I noticed the dirty blue cinder block walls when I walked back into my office. I cannot get away from that color. It reminded me of my dad's bedroom at home, the back room we called it. No one thought to paint it. His mother and father had taken him in, along with the three of us. That was all they were prepared to do. A wall was good for one thing—to hang up a shotgun.

I decided to paint the walls, put up some art; well, not real art. I had a Gaugin poster from the New Orleans Art Museum, three native women kneeling, looking straight ahead while preparing to look away. There was that Norman Rockwell reproduction, *The Problem We All Live With,* hanging in my guest room. It depicted Ruby Bridges, a six-year-old black child walking down the sidewalk in a pretty white dress to enroll in Franz Elementary School, two Federal Marshals in front of her and two behind. It was New Orleans in 1960 with anti-integration riots in the street right beside her.

Let me think about it. That print in my office might be inflammatory. Suddenly everything was about race. *Can't we all just get along?*

This school system cannot look away anymore. The Feds are here. Truth is, didn't I look away when blacks had to sit in the balcony at the fire station converted into the movie theater in Del City? Did I ever wonder why no black children came to swim in the public pool where I swam every day in the summer?

My body fell back into the smooth curve of the well-worn chair, shoulders relaxed. My first check will not come for a month and a half, something about the fiscal year. The $5200 is divided into twelve payments. At least Max and I can go out to eat the day I am paid, instead of having the regular: mayonnaisey tuna casserole with crackers on top. I will be glad when he gets out of pharmacy school. Then I'll have money to do anything I want! Maybe not anything; however, I will buy some new clothes and occasionally plan a steak and potato night.

I'm hungry right now. Why am I looking in this empty sack? I ate all the lunch I brought. Maybe somebody left a package of crackers in one of these drawers. Nope. Stripped. Remember? I think I saw a Nutty Buddy in that vending machine, bumpy chocolate with a current of caramel seeping through all those nuts, like on that billboard on I-10.

The paper was ripped off the candy bar and half of it gone before I got back to the office. *I remember eating these in high school.* I planned to save this second one, but—oink. Food was my default.

With my feet up on the desk to rest before the commute home, even a sugar high didn't give me the energy to move.

Static. *Maybe it's in my head.* Then a voice came through a speaker on the wall near the ceiling: "Mrs. Orchard? Mrs. Orchard? Mr. Ingleside wants to see you in his office before you leave the building today. Mrs. Orchard?"

"Yes, Ma'am."

Mr. Ingleside was busy when I walked into the office. Good. I'll have time to write down a few questions like, "How the hell could anybody learn to be a teacher under this kind of scrutiny? When anything you do could ruin your whole life—even with the friggin' government of the United States?" Asia, the answer to your question is, "No. No school prepared me to be a real teacher, not for this."

William Watson Purkey's book *Inviting School Success* changed the way I approached teaching, changed the way I approached students— the way I tried to approach life—forever. He suggests if a teacher creates an open, loving atmosphere; takes even a small success and builds upon it, then knowledge plus experience is delivered directly to the veins. I thought many times that first year Asia and others forgot to read their invitation from the Supreme Court and the Justice Department to leave their comfortable environment to attend Renville High.

Why is Asia on my mind? Because she was in my face all period. I asked her to be my assistant. I hope it works out. She straightened up for a few minutes before she began to let me know again what her grandma was and was not going to do. My dog's not in that fight. Blue, green, pink, or purple gym clothes, who cares? The students will wear what they've got for now.

"Welcome to your first assignment Mrs. Orchard. I peeked in on you today," Mr. Ingleside began.

"Yes sir." His eyes looked blood shot and his hair wasn't perfect. He must have had a day like mine. But… he was still smiling.

"Smile, Mrs.Orchard. It can't be that bad."

"Everything went okay for the first day, but I do have some questions."

"Fine, fine. As the Bible says, more will be revealed. Before we get down to business, do you two young people have a church home?"

"Uh. We recently married and moved here. Max drives back and forth to Monroe every day to pharmacy school. He'll be commuting in our little '62 Capri. I hope it runs all year."

"We'd like for you to visit us any Sunday over at First Baptist on Main Street. Wednesday night supper is tonight. Mary, my wife, makes the cornbread every week for the potluck, jalapeno bread. Have you ever made it?"

"My mother-in-law usually makes the cornbread."

It's four o'clock and I'm in overload. Will you please let me out of here?

"This is special. Here's the recipe. I give it to all the teachers."

Mary Ingleside's Jalapeno Corn Bread

Preheat oven to 425 degrees

Grease the skillet with bacon drippings or butter. Place it in the oven until sizzling hot.

Sift together:

¾ cup all-purpose flour

2 1/2 teaspoons baking powder

1 tablespoon sugar

¾ teaspoon salt

1 teaspoon soda

Add:

1 ¼ cups of stone-ground cornmeal

Beat in a separate bowl:

1 egg

Beat into it:
2 to 3 tablespoons drippings or butter from hot pan
1 1/3 cup buttermilk

Add:
1 8 oz. can cream style corn
2 whole jalapenos chopped fine
Combine ingredients and put batter in the hot pan. Bake 20 to 25 minutes.
(Rich brown crust and light, but slightly gritty bite.)

***To store your skillet, wipe it out with a damp cloth and give it a swipe with some lard to stay seasoned.

"Oh, thank you. I'll have to try it."

He looked at the picture of his wife on the desk and smiled with obvious satisfaction. "I wanted to talk to you today before you got off, about the basketball team. The girl's coach, Mrs. Orchard, will have an important part to play in this process we are in right now. I'll be honest with you, the Coloreds don't want to be here either. They have their own churches, schools. It is just a mess. They don't like these changes any better than we do, but they are here on us."

"I see." *Did he just say that? Does he realize he just invalidated anything more he has to say to me? He is the principal!*

"As it stands, there are two girls' varsity basketball teams."

"Pardon?"

"You will take the girls team from each of the high schools and put them together. You see, these girls all made the team in their respective schools. They all want to play. But, after thinking about this, I decided that the only fair way is to tell the girls that as of tomorrow, nobody has a position. We will have tryouts all over again when you're ready. Put the two teams together in a fair way, Mrs. Orchard. You know what I mean? And look, teach them how to get along, how to play together and get along."

"Yes sir." *He's undermining what we're doing and pretending to be the leader. I feel sick.*

"Now these girls have been rivals," he seemed amused, "so they probably don't like each other."

"When do you want to have tryouts?"

"As soon as possible. Are you okay, Mrs. Orchard? Mrs. Orchard? Marie, bring Mrs. Orchard a glass of water. You look a little pekid around the mouth."

"I'll be okay, thanks." *There's that pressure in my head. Breathe in ten. Out ten.*

"By the way, Mrs. Orchard, give Mary Cliff a call. She is a concerned parent; wants to know what position her daughter, Sandra, will play this year. Mrs. Cliff is secretary of the PTA, one of our good parents. Jack is a deacon in the church with me. Just give her a call. She wants to know if Sandra will be playing out front where she did last year. Here's the number."

"Yes sir. But, I don't know what to tell Mrs. Cliff."

"Tell her the truth," he said chuckling, "Tell her you are starting from scratch and will have tryouts on Friday."

"Yes sir. Will you be here? I mean on Friday?"

"I've got to go to Baton Rouge, but Mr. James will be somewhere around if you need him. Cheer up, Mrs. Orchard, You're doing a fine job, a fine job. It will get better."

"Yes sir."

"You be careful, very careful. Keep in touch with me. The way you handle this situation will keep us from having headaches down the road. Do you understand?"

"I understand. Some of the P.E. students have already complained that their mama can't afford the gold gym uniform."

"Well, don't worry about all those little things right now, Mrs. Orchard. People like to be with their own kind. Like I said, the government has gone to meddlin' where they have no business. But do not repeat me. Now what are your questions?"

"Ah, I understand. You answered my questions. Yes." *Now I know why he didn't have an assembly to share his beliefs about educational equality.*

What he does not understand is this: When the human spirit rises up, it cannot be stopped. He is right about one thing, a change is here on us—and it's bigger than he or I.

"Good, Good. If I don't see you tonight at prayer meeting, I will see you bright and early tomorrow morning. One more thing, Mrs. Orchard, you do know that my Jane will be trying out and the superintendent's daughter, Katherine, is on the team as well."

"Yes, Sir."

"How'd it go?" Max asked when I finally stepped into our rented mobile home—with a bay window. It was lovely.

"High school boys have their nerve, wolf whistling at a teacher! They wait until they're in a group so I can't tell who it is."

"You're smiling. Come on now."

"I'll never admit—I'm slightly flattered. I have to wear my white Bermuda shorts tomorrow. They look more like short shorts because my legs are so long. I'm concerned about what Mr. Ingleside will think. I can't afford new shorts until payday. I did find my wrap-around skirt in one of those boxes," I looked at the living room floor scattered with exhausted boxes. "The women have to wear a skirt over our shorts when we go out of the gym."

Max flipped through our checkbook, "We've still got a little money in the bank left from the honeymoon."

"I'm sure we do since you forgot to take any cash to Hot Springs and tried to starve me the first two days we were married; bread and bologna!"

Max looked at me with his little boy face, "How was I supposed to know we couldn't cash an out-of-state check? Don't you think it was kind of romantic, bread and water for two days? That will be another yarn for you to tell, Donna. You know how you like to chime in at a party and entertain with a good story, one that gets better with the tellin."

"Me? You know, honey," I put my arms around Max. "I thought about you working on that road crew this summer, the heat reflecting off of the highway, shoveling those high piles of asphalt, working like you've never worked before—so we'd have money to get married. I know you didn't have much choice."

"So much sweat ran down my face, my glasses kept falling off. The guys ragged me. Called me 'college boy' when they felt like being nice, but most of the time they called me, well, something foul-mouthed referring to my backside. Nobody even knew my name. They were good guys, though, worked hard. Moved from job to job following the road. I just wanted to get my time in, get my money, and get out of there."

I walked toward the kitchen, "What do you want for supper, honey? I forgot to thaw anything out. Looks like egg salad sandwiches again or maybe breakfast for supper with bacon, grits, and fried eggs?"

"Come sit down by me, Donna," Max said. "Don't worry about supper right now."

"Why are you looking at me that way, Max?" What's wrong with you? Is something wrong? I don't have to buy new shorts right now and..."

"I got my orders today."

"What?... You won't get commissioned until graduation at the end of next semester. I thought we would have at least two years here. You said they would probably wait a year to call you up."

"See." I looked at the papers.

"Upon graduation and commission Second Lieutenant ... will report to Fort Sam Houston Medical Service Corp by 2 May 1970."

"That's San Antonio," he said.

"Oh, I wasn't braced for this news, not today. Tell me you won't have to go to that awful war! Will you, Max?"

"No. None of my ROTC buddies called up this year were sent to Nam. There are peace talks in Paris. Nixon sent Kissinger. I hear it's about over. Honey, don't worry. I won't see combat."

"Are you sure? How can you be so sure?"

"Because, Donna, they're pulling troops. Only the Air Force is still being deployed. No army. People are marching on Washington, tired of this mess. You might as well finish out the school year. I'll be in basic."

"This is all so scary. Let me think about it, Max." I sat back down… "When I picked up my purse to head home from school today, I was called to Mr. Ingleside's office. I'm tired. I'll tell you about that later."

We come then to the question presented: Does segregation of children in public schools solely on the basis of race, even though the physical facilities and other "tangible" factors may be equal, deprive the children of the minority group of equal educational opportunities? We believe that it does.

Brown v Board of Education of Topeka 1954

Chapter 3

FUGITIVES FROM STUDY HALL

I could not escape my students in the little town of Renville, stumbling upon them in the grocery store, at church, at the one restaurant in town and shortly; they began dropping by my doublewide house trailer. There was some faux excuse, "I forgot to turn in my fundraiser money for the candy I sold." If I offered the kids a coke, they took that as an opportunity to ask personal questions, "When are ya'll going to have a baby?"

At school, the same four or five students appeared at my office door during their study hall or recess. I rolled my eyes and raised my eyebrow. "I don't want to be called up to the office by Mr. Ingleside for harboring fugitives from study hall. Here's a pass. Now get where you belong. And give me a couple of pieces of that chocolate you're eating."

Why do they think they can come to see me during a busy day?

When I got to Renville, Jeff Lowry's father was already confined to a wheelchair from Multiple Sclerosis, struck down by the disease in the midst of a successful high school coaching career. Everyone continued to call his dad 'coach.' When Jeff began to play football, the whole town shined a light on him. He was their darling. A muscular, handsome young man with clear blue eyes and black hair, he was charming and outgoing amid their absorption.

Katherine Fowler arrived at Renville High her junior year when her father was appointed superintendent of the Ryland Parish Schools. She balanced the equation, a tall beauty with thick brown hair and a warm smile—the football star and the superintendent's daughter. Jeff soon began asking Katherine to walk him off the field after the football game.

I taught boys and girls health class once a week down the hall in a classroom. Jeff began taking advantage of his *specialness* in his Southern, easygoing way. In other words, he tried to get me off the subject to get attention. I had seen it before and I was ready for him.

"How tall is your husband, Mrs. Orchard? Did he play sports?" Jeff blurted out in class.

"He's 6' 4 and no, he got an academic scholarship. And exactly what does that have to do with the definition of kinesiology, Jeff?"

"Kin…what? I guess it's something about our kinfolks," Jeff gets a big laugh from the class.

"Actually, you're right if your kinfolks move around a lot."

"Kinetic," Katherine speaks up. "Kinetic…energy. But I don't remember what it is."

"I've got you thinking now. You are getting warm. Kinetic energy is the energy that sets you in motion. You're on the right track. Would you believe it if I told you that you come into my clinic when you come to Physical Education? I measure your height and weight and give you a physical fitness test at the beginning and at the end of the year to help you set some goals, to see if there is improvement over the school year. We will run the mile and log it in, do pull ups. We play games and have lots of fun too. Come up to the front, Gene. I want to use you as an example." Gene was a hefty football player who didn't fit into his small student desk. I pulled a desk up and told him to sit down.

"There are other sciences that research motion and movement. Look at Gene, a big football player sitting in this desk. What's wrong?"

"He has to sit sideways in his desk. He doesn't fit." Gay Nell said.

"Yes. Write down this word, 'ergonomics.' This is a relatively new field. A specialist may come into the workplace to analyze the space in order to design an office to support a healthy body, through healthy movement. Research in this field may lead to suggestions like changing the chair in front of a typewriter to support the employee's back. Now let's get back to Gene."

"Yeah, tell Mr. Ingleside that all these desks are too little for me. My legs are all jammed up!"

"Exactly, Gene. Look, here's another teacher's chair. You can sit in this one for today. I'll try to find some larger desks before next week." I continued, "Now when you come to P.E. you know you're stepping into my clinic. And yes, I did have to go to school like any other teacher. You might say that I'm a clinical researcher."

"We know that. We like you. Most of our teachers been around here forever. You're going to stay aren't you Mrs. Orchard?" Jeff embarked on still another subject.

He couldn't know about Max's orders. Nobody here knows. I have to protect my job. I may be here next year if I can't join Max.

"Why wouldn't I stay? Okay. Let's move on. Where do most accidents occur?" I asked.

Jeff again, "Have you ever been injured Mrs. Orchard? I mean seriously? I got a concussion in football practice last week. Somebody rang my bell."

"What do you mean, *rang your bell*?" I frowned.

"That's what we say when we get hit and black out for a second or two, but it's nothing serious. I sat down for a few minutes."

"Oh, there's that other bell, the one to fourth period. We will talk more about that next week. Close your books. We'll be back in the gym tomorrow. Jeff, take the books up please and see me after class."

The last book was stacked as Jeff ran out of the door, "I know Mrs. Orchard. I'll do better next time."

Gee. I'm not going to run after him.

I'm concerned that I'm getting too chummy with the white students. They are often around my desk chatting. I have to be careful about that.

Except for Asia who was my assistant from the first day of school. Initially a survival tactic because of her quick wit, I was soon drawn to her. She was a little rough around the edges, raised by her grandmother, like I was. Her feisty sense of humor kept me from taking myself too seriously. Several times a day, in the morning, at lunch, at recess; I looked around and Asia was in my office filing papers, putting up equipment or sitting on my desk giving me the school buzz. I wondered about her family. She maintained a healthy relationship with her old friends and figured out how to make new ones. Nevertheless, she was not sure she was ready to go to a dance in the Renville gym on Friday night. I asked Jeff and Katherine if they would think about inviting Asia to go along with them. They didn't answer.

Donna, you are clearly out of line. Asia does not want to be taken on as a project.

That weekend I finally agreed to let Jeff and Katherine show me around the town—more like a village—on Saturday afternoon.

Two-Seed-in-the-Spirit Predestinarian Baptist Church on the edge of town was where we started, the first landmark for visitors driving into Renville from the college town of Monroe. The church was a little white house with shutters way too bright blue. The only indication that it was a church was a six-foot wooden cross out front, a white scarf hanging around the horizontal arms to the ground—and not just at Easter time. *They might change the color on those shutters with the money they save by not having missionaries*. They don't need them—missionaries I mean. Predestination. God already knows who's going to make it into heaven. Enter my anxiety. My childhood theology was changing; consequently, I was no longer sure if I was one of the *predestined* or even one of those *destined*...

Oh, I prayed. I knew that I was not God. When I was a kid, I prayed that Laddy, my dog, would not get mange because Daddy might take him far out on a dirt road, so far he could not find his way back home.

I prayed that Daddy didn't get drunk and miss Christmas.

Later I prayed that I would marry someone who didn't miss Christmas.

Jeff and Katherine pointed to their church, First Baptist, "where most people go." It was a typical Southern Baptist church building. Their members saved their money by not hiring architects. Every Southern Baptist church was a red brick office building, double glass doors, with a steeple stuck on top.

Unlike the Episcopal Church on the same street that had a red Spanish tile roof, a lovely gothic walk that surrounded a courtyard, and an arched passageway that led to the dark red doors at the entrance.

On the other end of Main Street was another red brick office building with a spire, the Second Southern Baptist Church.

Past the one red light in the center of town was Lucas Hardware Feed and Gun store, our first stop. Community notices were crowded in every space over the glass storefront.

"Dance at the Chicken Shack Friday night at seven o'clock featuring the Boogaloos, October 5, 1968." *That was last year.*

"Ask us about a Tupperware House Party."

"Bow season for doe begins this weekend."

"Is Mr. Boil here?"

The man in denim overalls at the counter put his hands on his hips and looked around. "No he must'a just stepped out, Jeff. By the way, your daddy called and needs this level. Let me charge that up, and you can take it with you." He cranked the handle on the invoice machine and rolled out a yellow copy on top. "Give this to Coach. You don't have to sign it."

I walked to the back past the compound bows, ammo and shotguns. "Is this a scale?" I called out to Jeff. " You could flop a big baby boy in there." I reached over to touch the smooth deep copper bottom of the oval scale, a lovely patina of dark brown in flashes of gold. "I'd like to put some flowers in this and put it at my front door."

"You can get up to five pounds of these nails," Jeff explained. "Find the size you need in this carrousel. There's everything in here from tiny picture nails to three inchers with heads almost as big as a dime, used to build houses."

The graduated nooks filled with thousands of nails readily became a repetitive piece of art in my mind's eye, a framed photograph. If I said such a thing to Emma—

my high school pal who was my flakiest friend by far—she'd tell me I was a photographer in my past life. I loved that about Emma.

"Watch me." Jeff reached for a huge rectangular magnet and poked it in a bin of big ones. Sticking in every direction on the end of the magnet, he held up the nails, a spiky porcupine. Then he released them with a crash into the bottom of the scale, as the weight on the side balanced for an accurate measurement.

"Who's Mr. Boil, Jeff?" I asked.

"Oh, 'Boil' is his nickname. That's Mr. Lucas who owns the store. I'll tell him you work at the school and he'll let you charge things you need. I don't know why they call him Boil. Somebody said it's because he likes to boil crawfish. I've also heard he had big sores on his neck when he was a kid."

When we got back into the car, I turned to Katherine and to my secret agenda. "I wish we could get more done at basketball practice, Katherine. Just when I think we're playing as a team, tempers flare again."

"Yes, Ma'am," she said embarrassed.

"I wish I had the answers. Thank you for doing your part in keeping things calm. Twenty-eight players are too many. That's one of the problems. Uh. This is an important time, an historic year of adjustment. It will get better. One day we will wonder what all this fuss was about. But today, it's hard. You and Jeff are warm and friendly. Just be yourselves. That's all anyone can ask of you."

The kids nodded in agreement. *I don't have the opening to spring into my lecture on racism*. They were spared for another day.

"Jeff, slow down. I saw an open-air market. Sure enough, spider lilies! They are 'pass-along plants' rarely seen in a nursery. The dark red spines cascade down to the stem, a burst of color in the spring, faithful year after year." *Way more than they wanted to know.*

As I put my plants in the car, "What's over there? The railroad tracks seem to run the full length of the town, like in Del City, my hometown."

"That's where the white middle schoolers have to go to school this year," Jeff waved his hand. "Glad it's not me. You don't want to go over there."

"I might!" I shot back before I had time to think.

My affection for my students was natural, if somewhat naïve, and soon gave rise to an uneasiness about how misleading that closeness could become. I had abruptly left my college friends when we moved to Renville and found myself newly married and often alone. Max was still in pharmacy school or working part-time in a drug store in another town.

The following Friday after the final bell, here they came to the gym: Asia and Gay Nell on the basketball team and of course Jeff and Katherine. *Don't these kids have something else to do?*

That's right, I remember that the football team has an open date this weekend. I've not heard of any problems with the foot-

ball team suddenly mixing the two high school teams. They probably butt heads in practice, literally, and deal with any of their aggressions that way, a blood sport. Maybe I should try that with the girls. Not really. I can feel the tension in the air when they get on the court. Latasha and Johnetta don't trust me. But why should they? That will take some time.

"Mrs. Orchard," Suzette walked into the office to find the other kids. "Mr. Ingleside is out in the gym looking for you,"

He was standing in the empty gym."Oh...Hi Mr. Ingleside."

"How's it going?"

"I'm glad it's Friday."

"Mrs. Orchard, I had a couple of your students come to my office with a complaint. I need to check this out with you. Two of the white girls tell me that you let the black students go to the bathroom, but refuse to let them go."

"Pardon? Let me think. I don't know what to say. Why would I do that? No, I have no idea what they're talking about. There are certain times when we're right at the end of the class and I ask them to wait a minute, but no. No. That is not true."

"Be careful, Mrs. Orchard. Treat everybody the same. I hoped there was nothing to it," he said with a pat on my back and a dour smile.

I felt negative energy when Mr. Ingleside was in my space—not lively kinetic energy that we talked about in class—but heavy and thick-bodied passiveness that turned me into little Donna who was afraid, gave up her right to breath his air.

Daddy will tell me, "This man's got you snake bit."

I walked back into my office. "Come here guys." I waved to the kids.

"Did he fuss at you?" Asia asked.

I ignored her. " I know most of you are going to the dance tonight and will be sleeping in, but I'll be up here painting my office tomorrow if you want to come and help. Look at this color for the walls, marigold yellow. It'll be cheery, don't you think?"

"It's bright," Asia caught herself. "Sure. I'll help paint. What time?"

"I'm like my Daddy and get up early if I've got a job to do. I will be here by seven o'clock. Come when you feel like it. I'll go to the Chicken Shack and get some fried chicken and onion rings for lunch."

Jeff picked up Katherine's hand, "We paint for chicken." He stopped and looked around, "My dad has paint brushes of all sizes. You'll need rags and a drop cloth, too."

I noticed my antique desk, "One of you grab the other side of the desk and help me move it out before you leave so I can start early. I don't want to drip on this."

"Katherine, pick up that desk," Jeff smiled at her. "Stand back girls. I can take it out by myself."

The next morning I painted half the office. The kids were sleeping late. When I got to the corner, I stood back to see if it was too bright. Too late now. One shade lighter... or darker would have been perfect. I know. I'll add some of this white trim paint to the yellow. Donna you are a genius. I will have to repaint the two walls I've finished. It's worth a try.

The kids can start on the white trim when they come—if they come. Should the trim be painted first? This scarf won't stay on my head. I reached up and pulled down a strand of hair, marigold yellow.

Painting is like cooking. You have to make a hideous mess to come out with something wonderful. Maybe not this hideous. Where is Jeff with those drop cloths?

Mrs. McConnell, my high school French teacher, designed her classroom like an outdoor Paris café. Exquisite. *Crème de café*? On Fridays we sat at small round tables and spoke French while we drank out of tea cups, ate squares of her chocolate cake— more like brownies—and used cloth napkins.

Mrs. McConnell's 30 Minute Chocolate Cake

2 c. flour 1 t. soda
2 c. sugar 1 t. vanilla
½ c. buttermilk 3 rounded T. cocoa
2 eggs 1 c. water
salt 2 sticks oleo (or butter)

Mix sugar and flour in a large bowl. In saucepan combine water, cocoa and oleo. Bring to boil. Pour over mixed flour and sugar. Mix well with hand mixer. Add eggs, buttermilk, soda, salt, and vanilla.

Pour into greased 11 x 16" pan. Bake 350 degrees 15-20 minutes. Spread with topping while still warm.

Topping:
1 stick oleo 1 t. vanilla
6 T. milk ½ c. pecan pieces
3 T. cocoa salt
1 box powdered sugar

Combine first 3 ingredients and bring to a boil. Turn off heat; Add sugar and vanilla and salt. Beat well; add nuts. Leave in pan. Slice as you use it.

This gym office will never look like Paris. I'll have to settle for too bright and a little less dirty blue. I glanced at my watch. It was 12:15. They are not going to come.

Shortly I heard a covey of voices and stuck my head around the door. There they were, all five of them: Katherine, Jeff, Asia, Gay Nell and Suzette.

"You didn't think we were going to come, did you Mrs. Orchard?" Asia said. "Hey you've got yellow hair!"

"Funny."

"We'll go get the chicken for you. Then we'll start. I'm starved," Jeff said. "Got some money?"

I looked back at the wall from outside the door. Still a tad too bright. That's what I get for criticizing the gaudy blue shutters at the little church on the edge of town. I better watch what I say about a church. God took offense at that comment and punished me with this marigold yellow.

I wonder what Jeff says to Katherine when she walks him off the football field on Friday nights after the game. When I was in high school, I sat in the stands with my baton on my lap and watched the couples arm in arm walk down the long field. I don't know, even now: *What's the big deal*? Maybe I will ask Katherine.

Asia did not mention the dance.

In the nature of things...commingling of the two races is unsatisfactory to either.

PLESSY V FERGUSON 1896

In approaching this problem, we cannot turn the clock back to 1868 when the (Fourteenth) Amendment was adopted or even to 1896 when Plessy v. Ferguson was written. We must consider public education in the light of its full development and its present place in American life throughout the Nation. Only in this way can it be determined if segregation in public schools deprives these plaintiffs of the equal protection of the laws.

BROWN V BOARD OF EDUCATION OF TOPEKA 1954

Chapter 4
THE MARSHALS

Just as I picked up the phone to dial Max and tell him to grab some take-out Chinese for supper, I looked up and there was Mr. Ingleside. *Uh. Oh.* Good-bye coconut shrimp.

"Mrs. Orchard, I came to tell you that one of the Marshals wants to meet with the two of us about the girls' basketball team. We want to ask you a few questions.

"What is this about?" I frowned.

"Everything will be all right. Don't get excited, Mrs. Orchard. Just answer the questions as truthfully as you can. We need to clarify some things. Walk down to my office with me."

"Clarify what things?" I probed.

"Be patient. Here we are."

Marie, the secretary, ducked her head as I walked by, no smile as usual. Mr. Ingleside opened his door and motioned for me to sit at the round table with him and one of the Marshals, easily recognizable, never in their shirtsleeves, always a jacket.

"How was your day? Mrs. Orchard?" Mr. Ingleside began.

"Just fine now that the week is over," I said as we all smiled.

"Mrs. Orchard, this is Mr. Coleman with the Justice Department. I'm sure you have seen him around the building." He stood and we shook hands.

"Yes, Sir. Can't miss them." My dismal attempt at cheerfulness made me more insecure.

"Mrs. Orchard," the principal began, "It has come to our attention that you talked to the black players and the white players separately, divided them by race..."

"Before we go any further," Mr. Coleman interrupted and turned off the tape recorder, "Mrs. Orchard I would like to record our conference. Are you in agreement? Please speak into the microphone." He turned on the recorder.

After you read my Miranda rights and allow me to have my attorney present.

"Mrs. Orchard?" Mr. Coleman prompted me.

"Uh, yes."

"Today is October 7, 1969, and I am Marshal Clarence Coleman in the office of Mr. Frank Ingleside, principal of Renville High School in Renville, Louisiana. Seated with us is gym teacher and coach, Mrs. Donna Orchard. It is 4:15 p.m." He turned off the recorder again, "I apologize for the interruption. Let's start again Mr. Ingleside."

The recording continued. "It has come to our attention, Mrs. Orchard, that you talked to the girls on the basketball team separately, divided by race."

"Are the facts correct so far, Mrs. Orchard?" asked Marshal Coleman.

"Yes." *I must have done something terrible. I thought I was doing my job by keeping them from coming to blows. There are all of these unwritten rules that everybody seems to know—except me.*

"Explain the situation to us, would you?" Mr. Ingleside did the questioning.

"Let me tell you what I was up against. All of the players were chosen at their respective schools to be on the varsity team last year before the consolidation was announced. I was instructed by Mr. Ingleside to have tryouts again and come up with one team. With few exceptions, all of the girls on both teams tried out. I did not want to travel with such a large number of girls, but I did not see how I could cut players who were already chosen for a team. It was a no-win situation. Claims of racism from both groups would have cast a shadow over any decision I made. The tryouts pitted the players against one another and increased the rivalry for each position. I have twenty-eight girls on the team. An average team is about fifteen girls. Tuesday at practice the girls began squabbling again about who would be the starters for the first game. Some of the girls are seniors and have had their position for three years. Suddenly a loose ball sparked their anger. Kathy got in Latasha's face about who would take the ball out on the sidelines.

I sat them on the bench, but they would not let it go. Kathy was so mad that she was white around the mouth. I told them all to sit down on the floor in a group."

Mr. Ingleside doesn't seem to be listening. I saw him look at his watch.

"I looked up, and rushing in the door was Kathy's mother. She came in unannounced to ask me if Kathy would play forward, bring the ball down the court like she had for the last three years. Latasha was still angry and started yelling at the parent to leave. Then Kathy's mother yelled back, 'My baby's played her position for three years,' and moved toward Latasha. Latasha stood up. At this point, I told the black girls to go back to the dressing room. I moved closer to the mother, who was quit large, in case I had to restrain her. I asked her come outside with me and let me handle the girls. Thankfully, she did calm down when we got out into the hall and she left the building.

I talked to the white players in the gym and then went into the back and talked to the other group to find the underlying cause of the threats and name-calling. I told both groups the same thing: We will not have a team at all if the disruption continues."

Mr. Ingleside will never call off the season when his daughter Jane is the star player. That will never happen.

Mr. Ingleside said, "Mrs. Orchard, don't ever talk to your group separately, separated by race. Always talk to the girls together. I do not think that you meant any harm; let me say that. However, the way you handled this situation could breed mistrust. Keep the whole group together so that everyone hears the same thing."

"I understand that I did something very wrong. No, I will never do that again. Not again..." I started crying. "Mr. Coleman, I respect all of my girls. I was just trying to talk some sense into them. That's all. We can't start the season with all this tension and expect to play as a team. We have two months until the first game and..."

"I hear you, little lady," Marshal Colman's tenor changed." Now take this tissue and dry your eyes. This is not going to affect your employment. Mr. Ingleside and I are here to help you. Let me know if you see improvement in the next few weeks, as they settle in, Mrs. Orchard."

"If they are still at each other's throats, I think we will have to call off the season." I said.

"Oh, no, that will not happen," Mr. Ingleside answered quickly. "We will play. The schedule is agreed upon." He made that clear. "Cheer up. You're doing a fine job, a fine job. It will get better."

"Yes, sir."

The principal looked at the clock, "I see that it is 5 o'clock, and it's Friday. We are all tired. Do you have any more questions, Marshal?"

"No." Mr. Colman looked at me. "I know you're doing the best you can, little lady."

As I turned and rushed out of the door, I realized that the Marshal had stood up and offered his hand.

When I got out into the hall, the other two government men were talking.

One turned around, "Hi Miss. I'm Lonnie Marshall. You can go ahead and laugh. That's my real name. I want to ask some of you teachers how you think the changes are proceeding. What's your name?"

"Donna Orchard. Right now, I don't feel like much of a teacher. Is your report going to somebody important, like to the President of the United States? Somebody's already beat you to that one a few minutes ago."

"No. Stop just a minute Ma'am. Settle down."

"Yes, the changes. Well, I'm new. First year. This is a good school. No, no real problems yet. It's a good, smooth ...."

Pushing the door open, a sharp pain went up my arm—*no time to be sick ever again with the rent due next week.* Bragging about not having any backup didn't feel as romantic as it did when I was in college. Get out of school in four years and get a job obsessed me. I ignored most of the Vietnam War for god's sake. Going back home was not an option. Nobody was going to send money in a pinch. Max's parents didn't have money either. What about my stubborn belief that a teaching certificate would always enable me to make a car payment and pay the rent? Who would think about being sick or simply feeling beat down?

Some rest will make a difference—Drama Queen.

We conclude that, in the field of public education, the doctrine of "separate but equal" has no place. Separate educational facilities are inherently unequal. Therefore, we hold that the plaintiffs and others similarly situated for whom the actions have been brought are, by reason of the segregation complained of, deprived of the equal protection of the laws guaranteed by the Fourteenth Amendment. This disposition makes unnecessary any discussion whether such segregation also violates the Due Process Clause of the Fourteenth Amendment.

BROWN V BOARD OF EDUCATION OF TOPEKA 1954

Chapter 5

A LONG ROAD TRIP

Monday Morning

"Mrs.Orchard I've been sent to hold your class while you go to the office"

"Hi, Ms. Marie." She looked at me with understanding "Who wants to see me?"

"Mr. Ingleside. You can go on in."

"Hi, Mrs. Orchard, how did things go Friday night?"

"They got along surprisingly well on the long trip up to Delta. They've decided that the song "White Christmas" is their good luck song—even though it's February. All of the girls sang on the bus, both verses:

I'm dreaming of a la la la

Then, with every card... They've decided to sing their song in the dressing room before every game. I thought that was a good sig...."

"Okay, Okay, Mrs. Orchard. How about the game?"

"We lost 32-17." *I gasped when I forget to breathe.* "We did have some trouble on the bus coming home."

"Yes, Kathy Lamar's father called me at home this weekend. Said a colored girl, Latasha, hit Kathy."

"I talked to Mr. Lamar Friday night when he picked Kathy up from the school. I told him I was sorry this happened and that we would get to the bottom of it today. I didn't see who threw the first punch. The kids say Kathy did. Mr. Lamar said he'd be up here today."

"What was it about, Mrs. Orchard? I mean what caused them to get into it?"

"I talked to Kathy and Latasha on the way to the game when I got wind that the bad blood between them the week before was still simmering. Frankly, I think they just don't like each other. Latasha dribbles the ball around the court so she won't have to pass to Kathy. The girls say Kathy started the cursing again on the way back home."

"I waited for Latasha's mother Friday night and talked to her too. She was upset and afraid that Latasha would be suspended. I told her probably so. 'Anytime there is a fight, both students are suspended. Students cannot put their hands on each other.' They should have come to me before they came to blows. I was sitting in the front about four seats in front of them."

"I know girls care more about their cat fights than winning the game," Mr. Ingleside gave me his disgusted look with his gnarly fingers on his chin. "Those girls don't want to be over here. They don't get in as much playing time. Be sure they all get to play, Mrs. Orchard. By the way, the boys are doing pretty well. They just want to win basketball games."

"Yes, Sir. I finished the two discipline reports with a list of witnesses. I don't know who started the fight.

It's hard to say. They were all yelling. The kids say suddenly Kathy slapped Latasha in the face so hard she fell down into the aisle. I saw Kathy kicking her, stomping on her face. They were out of control. Neither one of them seemed to hear me when I yelled, 'Stop!' Boys will usually stop when they hear my voice. Not girls. I got Kathy around the waist and dug my heels in to pull her off of Latasha. There was lots of cursing, the 'F' word. Kathy was able to reach her leg out to kick Latasha several more times as I dragged her down the aisle. Mr. Flynn, the bus driver, couldn't get through to help me. One of the girls jumped up and grabbed Latasha. She has a bump on her head and they are both scratched up, but there were no serious injuries. I don't want either one of them back on the team."

"Now we can't do that, Mrs. Orchard, but I'll do an investigation. They won't be at practice today. I'll talk to their parents and cool their heels at home for a few days".

I sat in my old oak swivel chair at lunch and reflected on the turn of events—the ones that landed me in this particular time and place. Civil rights. I cannot look to anyone else. Many courageous people have cut a swath to this path, to put us where we are today. I cannot disappoint. We have to move forward.

I am not courageous. I am mostly panicked and terrified. I don't remember signing up for...courageous.

Maslow's hierarchy. My physical safety was suddenly at risk as the fight broke out, then a surge of fear came up in my throat. I managed to act on instinct before I collapsed. Fear defaulted to anger.

My mind started to swing full tilt to the other career choices I might have made. If I had garnered the will-power to go on a crash diet, I could be on an airplane right now headed to some exotic European city, to Paris and Montmartre, where Picasso painted and writers gathered...airline stewardess. *I want to be anywhere but here.*

I thought about my girls. Once students were on my class role, I considered them mine. *I want them to be happy. I want us to be happy.*

When the basketball team came in that afternoon, the first thing out of their mouth was, "What happened to Kathy and Latasha?"

"Girls, we need a break," I pulled them into a circle close around me. "I'm giving you the day off." There was an unrestrained yelp of approval. "How many of you like Stevie Wonder?" Every hand went up. "Coach Terry agreed to let us have class today in the weight room, mirrors on every wall. The boys are out on the football field sixth period. I'll show you some jazz routines and you can show me some of your dance steps. Let's go to the weight room and dance!"

There was another loud roar, "Yes!" as Asia jumped up to do the mashed potato.

We looked around the large room and pushed the benches out of the way. "This is going to be our dance studio. Dance will help you with balance and flexibility on the basketball court." *If Mr. Ingleside comes in, he'll wonder what we're doing. Baptists don't like dancing.*

While I put the LP on the stereo, the girls wiggled, pranced, and laughed at themselves in the mirrors that reached the ceiling.

I smiled inside. "My cheri amour pretty little girl that I adore..."

Chapter 6

LOOSEN UP THAT CORSET

The basketball team pulled the balls out of the mesh bag and were soon sweaty, taking some shots, when I walked out from the back to center court, "Come sit on the bench, girls."

They stopped and looked at me, "Whatcha wearing, Mrs. Orchard?" Lilly giggled.

"I'll get to that in a minute. A couple of you help me pass out your notebooks and pencils."

The moans reverberated out to me, "We are ready to scrimmage today!" Katherine complained.

"I'll pass 'em out." Asia said.

"Have you ever wondered about the first person who put up a net and threw a round ball through a hoop?" I waved my arm around to the basketball goal. "How many of you know who invented the game of basketball?"

No response.

"A man invented the game at the end of the Nineteenth Century, Dr. James Naismith. In 1891, Naismith's boss at the YMCA in Massachusetts got an idea. Because the winters were so long and bitter, he asked Dr. J—--that's what he was called—to invent an indoor activity to keep the young boys active when they couldn't go outside. You know how rambunctious the boys are in here on rainy days. You girls sit on the bleachers while the boys run up and down the basketball court."

"I think we should get to play on rainy days too!"

"I know Becky. Give me some time to talk it over with the coaches. I'm new here, you know."

"This is going to be *borr ring."* Cindy looked down the row at the other girls.

I tapped my foot, impatiently, "Cindy don't you think Asia owns that word?" Asia smiled. "And no, the history of our game is anything but borr-ring. The history of women's basketball is exciting, sad, funny and guess what? We are still making history. I read that in some colleges today women play by men's rules, five players, full court."

"Whoa! But why you got on a long dress? Wait. I know. You're probably going to a party with Mr. Ingleside!" Asia laughed.

"Guess what the first women basketball players wore?" Arms shot up.

"Baggy shorts." One shout.

"No, long pants. "Another shout.

"Not even close. Not at first," I said. "Pardon me while I loosen my corset. That's better. A girl's got to be able to breath."

Gay Nell frowned, "What's a corset?"

Jennifer leaned over to look at me from the back row, "It's one of those tight things women wore under a dress to make their waist look little. They tied it up in the back."

"Yes, Jennifer. Exactly. Can you imagine moving around on the basketball court bound in a corset? Proper women in the 1890s wore these floor length dresses." I twirled around in my green and gold plaid dress with white Peter Pan collar and fitted bodice. "Everywhere—including the basketball court—a woman's body was essentially held secret from the public eye; only their fingers, necks and heads could be exposed."

"I hate dresses, but Mama makes me wear 'em to church," Debra said.

"We live in the South," I responded, "where female customs change slowly and women's basketball is steeped in tradition, some of it humorous to us today, but fascinating. When I went to college at Northeast in Monroe, right down the road, I had to wear a raincoat over my shorts to walk across campus to my gym classes."

"That's not fair, Mrs. Orchard. Coach Terry and the other men coaches wear their shorts into the front office. I see them."

"I don't mind wearing my wrap-around skirt when I go out into the hall, Paula. We'll get back to that. Okay. Look at me... What do you think happened when girls played in these long dresses?" I pulled out the cascading skirt and pushed up my sleeves.

"Are you going to play in that, with those little flats on?" Kate asked.

"I'm going to dribble the ball down the court in a run and shoot a crib shot. Watch."

"Go, go, go, go..." they yelled.

"Whoa!!! You almost fell when you jumped to rebound the ball and you stepped on your dress! You missed too!"

"Exactly, Katherine. There were broken bones and black eyes. Can you imagine trying to pivot wearing a long dress, a petticoat and pink slippers with rosettes?"

"Some man made up those rules!"

"No, Johnetta. College women began playing basketball less than a year after this new game was invented. Senda Berenson, a gymnastics instructor at Smith College in Massachusetts read an article by Dr. Naismith and wondered if the game would be good for girls. That was thirty years before women suffrage, before women got to vote."

"Oh we studied about that. White men had the right to vote, then black men, then women. We were last," Debra looked around at the other girls.

"Did I see a paper wad fly through the air?! "I asked.

Asia added, "They are throwing pencils up here too."

"Okay, girls. Plan on a 100-point test tomorrow. And, you will not leave today until all the trash is picked up under the bleachers."

"That white woman's crazy." I couldn't see where that came from.

"Let's get back to the lesson." I gave them my evil eye. "If women coaches suggested that we could play a man's game like a man, it would have outraged men and women alike." I chuckled to myself when I thought about Max. "When I sat on the couch at home last night preparing for this lesson, I began cackling out loud. My husband, Max, was curious and asked me what was so funny. In the late 1800s most people thought if women exercised they would get the torpors, or the vapors, and fall to the floor in a swoon and have to be revived with salts."

"I can beat my twin brother running a sprint." Lucy was outraged.

"Yes, Lucy, I want you to see how far girls have come. Women were thought of as weak and submissive. We thought of ourselves that way. Even Berenson worried that girls might suffer from nervous fatigue if games were too strenuous. She adapted the rules to make it easier for women to play. The court was divided into three sections and required the women to stay in their place, pardon the pun."

"What's a *pun*?" Katherine frowned.

"Let me see how can I explain that to you…A pun is a humorous use of a word that could have two meanings. 'To put a woman in her place' could mean to keep her in the home and may suggest that women should not work. In this context, I was talking about their position on the basketball court. On the other hand, a pun might be something that causes deliberate confusion, like, 'I'm going to sit on this notebook on the history of women's basketball so you can't get me off the subject!' I will give you an extra ten points on Friday if you bring in a pun and we'll share them. Now. Let's get back on the subject."

They laughed and sat on their notebooks.

"There would be no snatching the ball, holding it for more than three seconds or dribbling it more than three times in the modified rules for women. These rules were enforced to prevent a young lady from developing *dangerous nervous tendencies and losing the grace and dignity and self-respect we would all have her foster."* The girls snickered.

"Guess what? Women in the Middle East in the Sixth Century invented trousers for themselves many years before men started wearing pants. Men didn't start wearing trousers until conquering Persians took them from the women. When we started wearing pants, we were just taking back what belonged to us in the first place!"

"Men wore dresses and women wore pants? I'd like to see Mr. Ingleside in a dress!" Asia, of course.

"Come on girls." I said. "It didn't take long for the basketball coach at Sophie Newcomb to introduce bloomers with a split in the middle so her players could get around safely. That was an important change for women players. You can imagine. Sophie Newcomb College is right here in our state, in New Orleans. Their women's basketball team was one of the first four organized in the U.S."

I let it slip that women coaches at the high school level were volunteers.

"You mean you don't get paid?" Lilly asked.

"That is personal. Yes, I am paid a teacher's salary. My point is that these women recognized that one of the most common arguments against giving women equal pay at work was that they were prone to illness. What is another reason why women don't get equal pay?" I asked.

"They can't go to work if their babies are sick." Paula answered.

"Absolutely, Paula, yes, but before that, they get pregnant. They have to be off the job to have the babies."

"You don't get paid for coaching basketball or for following the cheerleaders around, Mrs. Orchard?"

"It is complicated isn't it? Remember I told you that Berenson realized that when women demonstrated that we were strong on the playing fields, we would then lead the way to equal pay for equal work. Listen to this. Women's rules became even stranger. No sooner had basketball taken hold in women's colleges that an outcry was raised that it was eroding sacred concepts of womanhood. A newspaper article stated that previously well-bred young ladies could be seen running and falling, shrieking in excitement and, worst of all, calling each other by nicknames."

"Yo, Princess. That's my nickname," Asia yelled.

"I know, Asia. Are you sure your nickname is not *borring*? Just kidding. I like Princess. It fits you."

She smiled at me.

"Games would end with handkerchiefs and hairpins scattered all over the gym floor. One article in the Los Angeles Times had a headline: '*Sweet Things Have Scrap.*'

The reporter wrote: *There was something disquieting in the grim and murderous determinations with which the young ladies chased each other all over the court."*

I cautioned my girls. "By the way, if you start hair pulling, you are on the bench for the rest of the game. The second time, you are suspended. No. No hair pulling on my team."

"That girl pulled my hair Friday night!" Carol yelled.

"I didn't see that."

"She may not have meant to. My hair is long,"

"Let me just say for the record that a good game of basketball never put me in as grim and murderous a mood as a patch of needlework did," Sally Jenkins wrote in *The History of Women's Basketball.* The girls didn't catch the humor.

"Are we gonna have a test on this?"

"Obviously you weren't listening, Robin. We will have a test when you come in tomorrow. I'll find out who was taking notes. We'll meet in the health classroom to take the test."

I continued, "More restrictions were proposed for girls to make the game more compatible with popular views of a woman: *neatly combed hair, no gum chewing or slang, never calling each other by last names and never lying or sitting down on the floor."*

"We'd get kicked out of every game," said Jenny, "I have to chew gum when I'm nervous."

Lilly pointed out that 'Ingle' is what we call Jane Ingleside.

"How many of you like to look beautiful?" I looked up and smiled at the lovely young girls on the bleachers. Most of their hands went up. "Yes, men still wanted women to be beautiful—even though they were playing basketball—and we cared about our appearance too. At the same time, women were gaining recognition as athletes. How would you like to dye your hair red to play basketball?"

"That would be fun!" they grinned.

"A group of gifted women called 'The Red Heads' toured the country playing exhibitions against men's teams. Team members were required to wear makeup, look beautiful and play well. They were also required to either wear red wigs or, get this, dye their hair red. That's right."

The girls whooped.

"Okay, now let's come up to how we play the game today. You know we have two roving forwards today who can go up and down the court. When I was in high school, just four years ago, we played six on one end of the court and six on the other. We all stayed in our place. I played guard for four years and never took a shot in a game."

"That's not fair. What if you were fouled?"

"Good question, Katherine. I gave the ball to one of my teammates to shoot my free throw on the other end of the court."

"That would be *borr ring.* You did weirdo things back in that day," Kathy said, "that's the reason all of us want to play rover so we can snatch the ball anywhere on the court and drive down for a shot."

"And you're good at that, Kathy" then mumbled to myself, "a *way to harness all that aggression.*"

"What?"

"Oh, nothing. Sometime I talk to myself."

"That's what old people do, Mrs. Orchard," Cindy teased.

I continued with the history of the sport, "There is no reason why we should not open up the court for girls and play by men's rules, five players and full court. Women are ready. That will come next."

"Dr. J, the inventor of basketball had a nickname," Carol said thoughtfully.

"I never made that connection, Carol. You are right."

"Let's call him up."

"A loud roar of laughter."

"He's dead crazy girl," Johnetta reminded Paula.

"Oh yeah." she giggled at herself.

"I've got to run to the back and get something. Stay seated." I waved my hand for them to stay put.

I walked out from the back carrying a big box. "Our new uniforms finally came in!"

I heard a loud, "Finally!"

As the first names and numbers were called, the girls held up their shiny satin suit for all to see.

"Too bad the ladies back in the day didn't have these gold shorts. Look at mine." Gay Nell held up her shorts.

"I like the white stripes down the side. But my name's not on the back of my top like the boys."

"There'll be many more girls who wear your uniform after you leave, so we put 'Hornets' on the back."

When I stepped into the trailer that afternoon, Max asked, "Did the girls like their new uniforms?"

"Oh, man, did they! The girls were finally happy for a few minutes. It made me feel good. They needed that. I needed that. The thick, well-made shorts won't show their panty line. They are so much better than those old white—those dingy white ones. Mr. Ingleside reminded me that we would have to use the new ones for several years. I told the girls to be careful with them when they wash them and 'don't lose your uniform because you won't get another one.' Speaking of Mr. Ingleside, when I was leaving today, it was late—with fitting the uniforms and everything—and he waved me into his office."

"Uh-oh."

"He reminded me that he talked to me Friday before I left for that game with Lynberg. He told me that it was a rough school and to lock the dressing room door to protect the girls' personal belongings every time I went out into the gym. He did tell me right before we left to *lock the door.* Fear does something to my brain, honey. I don't use good judgment."

Max just looked at me, knowing that I wanted him to just listen."Mr. Ingleside found out that some of the girls lost their money and asked me what happened. I was so embarrassed. I felt like a stupid dumb ass! I told him the truth, that they were angry because they were losing at half time and were blaming each other. They were about to come to blows when I pushed them out the door and back into the gym. I just forgot to call somebody over to lock the door, Max. It was my luck that somebody came in and stole their money. I was keeping my fingers crossed that he wouldn't find out. I was going to replace the money myself…and…"

"Come here, honey. You're in a very difficult spot. You are going to make mistakes. He should be glad somebody is willing to take that job! A volunteer coach, out until ten and eleven o'clock at night for that little bit of money. Don't worry about it."

"He might fire me, hon."

"Let him. I've got my orders."

"I can't just leave my job. Where would we get money?" I started to cry. "Anyway, I told him I would replace any money that the girls lost and he told me not to worry about it. I'm just a dumb ass, Max. He gave me specific instructions about the door and I could not do *that one thing*. What's wrong with me?"

"Honey, you are under a tremendous amount of pressure—from the students, the principal, the school board and the parents—oh, I forgot the Federal Marshals. I would not have your job. The only mistake I can make in the pharmacy is to possibly kill somebody if I give them the wrong drug."

"That's the only bad thing Mr. Ingleside hasn't blamed me for—yet." I stayed in Max's arms until my tears turned to giggles.

The effect of this separation on their education opportunities was well stated by a finding in the Kansas case (Plessy v Ferguson) which nevertheless felt compelled to rule against the Negro plaintiffs:

Segregation of white and colored children in public schools has a detrimental effect upon the colored children. The impact is greater when it has the sanction of the law, for the policy of separating the races is usually interpreted as denoting the inferiority of the Negro group. A sense of inferiority affects the motivation of a child to learn. Segregation with the sanction of law, therefore, has a tendency to (retard) the educational and mental development of Negro children and to deprive them of some of the benefits they would receive in a racial [ly] integrated school system.

BROWN V. THE BOARD OF EDUCATION OF TOPEKA 1954

Chapter 7

BROWN V. THE BOARD

Imagine Linda Brown, a seven-year-old, walking one mile to a bus stop by going through a railroad switching station and then waiting for a school bus to go to a black elementary school. There was a white elementary school only seven blocks away. This is what happened to the third grader from Topeka, Kansas.

Oliver Brown and thirteen other parents tried to enroll their children in the local white schools. They were told their children must attend one of the four schools in the city for African American children. Oliver Brown is the first parent listed in the lawsuit, therefore, the case is named after him.

At the time of the lawsuit, blacks everywhere are not treated fairly. For every $150.00 spent on white children at the white schools, only $50.00 is spent on African American children at the black schools. The parents of the African American children discover that their schools are not treated equally because they are Colored. They do not have the most current textbooks or enough school supplies and they have overcrowded classrooms.

The US Supreme Court used the Clark Study in the 1940s to help support their decision to declare segregation in public schools unconstitutional.

The Clarks, African-American psychologists, on the cusp of the civil right movement, conducted social and psychological research on African-American schoolchildren. In their study, Kenneth and Mamie Clark used a pair of black and white baby dolls to study African-American children's perceptions of their own race. The study comprised two groups: one group attended integrated schools, the other segregated schools.

In the experiment, African-American children aged six to nine were given the two dolls to play with. The Clarks noted sixty-three percent of the children preferred the white doll. When asked questions about which doll was good, and which doll was bad, most identified the white doll as "good" and the black doll as "bad." The Clarks concluded from these and other experiments over time that the children in segregated schools had internalized white society's negative stereotypes of African-Americans, damaging their self-image as worthwhile people.

Chief Justice Earl Warren wrote in the decision:

"...Such considerations apply with added force to children in grade and high schools. To separate them from others of similar age and qualifications solely because of their race generates a feeling of inferiority as to their status in the community that may affect their hearts and minds in a way unlikely ever to be undone."

After three long years, the case finally ended on May 17, 1954 with the court finding in favor of Linda Brown and the other African-American children. The judges voted nine to zero.

"No matter how much the Supreme Court seeks to sugarcoat its bitter pill of tyranny, the people of Georgia and the South will not swallow it."

GEORGIA GOVERNOR MARVIN GRIFFIN

It took some states many years to implement fairness to all students. Integration was more complicated in the South where half the population of many cities and towns were African American. The power struggles remain today, where de facto segregation is not uncommon in community housing and schools.

'Coloreds' was commonplace when I grew up in North Louisiana in the 50s and early 60s.

In 1851, The New York Times referred to a 'colored population' and around that same time, the War Department established the 'Bureau of Colored Troops.'

The National Association for the Advancement of Colored people, commonly known as the NAACP, issued a statement concerning the word 'colored,' in 2008, "It's outdated and antiquated, but not offensive. The name was chosen because it was the most positive description commonly used in 1909 when the association was founded."

In 1966, 'Negro' was how most black Americans described themselves. A year later with the release of Stokely Carmichael's book, *Black Power: The Politics of Liberation in America;* 'black' became the preference.

Jesse Jackson led the push for 'African-American' instead of 'black' in the 80s, however, it never completely took hold and most publications do not recommend one over the other.

Michelle Obama recently voiced her preference for 'people of color' since all blacks are not from Africa.

Chapter 8

BEFORE AUTOMATIC WASHERS, DRYERS AND PERMANENT PRESS

"I'm gonna sit at the welcome table." I heard a haunting melody coming from a little chapel in Montogomery, Alabama, while I was strolling a book festival in 2008. Then the final lyrics, "I'm gonna sit at the Woolworth counter (and eat!) one of these days." The duet was sung by Guy and Candie Carawan, civil rights activists in the 60's. They were one of the two writers responsible for the moving, "We Shall Overcome."

I was different, the only kid in Del City who lost her mother and couldn't find her.

Ineey, meeny, mineey, mo, catch a n------by the toe, if he hollers, make him pay, fifty dollars every day. My - mother - told - me - to - choose - this - one. The captain pointed his finger down the line. This is how we chose teams for a baseball game in the patch, a dusty field down the hill from where I lived. I was the only girl. I could run fast in my yellow and brown plaid dress tied in the back, short waisted for a tall eight-year-old—a hand-me-down. Barefoot for the summer with dirty toenails, I was chosen for the team before the scrawny boys. I had a good arm.

This was my life.

Del City, my hometown in North Louisiana, is in the piney woods near the Arkansas state line. In college my speech teacher was determined that my pronunciations would morph from Southern sorghum into nondescript Midwestern. I could see his enthusiasm waning when I couldn't distinguish 'pin' from 'pen.' He finally decided he was wasting his time, gave me a 'C' and allowed me to languish without hope of becoming a Chicago newscaster.

My small town of 5000 residents is isolated on the Minden Road, fifty miles from Shreveport, the nearest large city. You don't run up on Del City when you are headed someplace else.

Coming into town on the right, was the only factory, a timber processing plant, and shortly the sign, "Welcome to Del City, a fine place to live."

Just inside the city limits was the Purple Cow Café that served burgers in red baskets under piles of onion rings. Rounding the curve was a car repair shop with a pile of rusty cars out front. Next was the Louisville & Nashville Railroad (L & N) that revived Del City after the Civil War. The tracks ran the length of the town carrying travelers and cargo north.

I was three years old when I first rode into Del City on that Minden road, all the way from Cincinnati, not on one of those trains, but in Big Papa's black Studebaker. Daddy snatched us in the middle of the night and stuffed the three of us: Marilyn, nine, Jimmy, seven, and me into the back seat. A vigilant child, I knew even at three, that my mother was too sick to take care of us.

When the car finally stopped, Big Papa got out still wearing his suit and tie. I had sat in the back seat behind him all the way from Cincinnati. I looked up at him. He had red hair, square jaws and a big nose. I knew immediately that he was the boss of this family.

About that time Granny, my grandmother, burst out of the door. She was all round with soft, flappy arms that went around me twice. A fine hair net covered her white hair that was mostly blue. I smelled Coty face powder, the same kind my mother used. I could tell that my grandmother was more of a girly girl than I was. Her face was clear and rosy, wire eyeglasses on her nose. She fidgeted with her orange and yellow flowered housedress, a sweet ruffled collar at the neck with white tatting around the edges. Her hug went on way too long.

Granny raised me after my mother became mentally ill, but it was Ida Champ, our Colored maid, who slowed down long enough to hold me during the day after her ironing and cooking were done.

I didn't know where we got the money to pay Ida. We didn't have extras, like meat—except on Sunday—or orange juice for breakfast. Daddy made good money as a roughneck in the oilfields of North Louisiana and East Texas so I suspect he paid Miss Ida.

My grandmother needed some help after Jim showed up at her door with three more young'uns for her to raise. We were numbers eleven, twelve and thirteen. Only seven of the kids were Granny's own children. The rest of us were strays, whom she got by default, when someone got divorced, or someone like my mother—they whispered—had a 'nervous breakdown.'

Ida Champ wore a white maid's uniform with a red bandana tied around her thick black hair that bunched up through a hole in the top. I followed her around while she ironed, cooked and dusted—pulled on her dress tail.

At dinner time, our big meal in the middle of the day, if Ida didn't see me, she'd open the back screen door and call, "Ya hoo, Donna!"

Oh, man. I bat next. She always calls when it's my bat!

My little high-water dress was smeared by now with red clay from sliding into base. When I hit the door, one of the sashes ripped off, Ida put the iron down sudden and deliberate to look at me for the longest, "Child, child, what a sight! You'sa little girl. You just won't do."

The small red stool in the kitchen was my way to spy on adults, to listen for signs of trouble without being noticed. I pulled the stool up to the kitchen counter and ate beside Ida. She looked to the ceiling, thinking, trying to decide what she was going to cook for her family that night, "collard greens with ham hocks, meat loaf and a double pone of bread." I liked Ida's thin cornbread, soft inside with a crispy buttery crust. After she put the leftovers on the stove for supper and washed the dinner dishes, she sat down in a rocking chair in the breakfast room, my signal to jump up into her lap. No stories or songs. She rocked and held me, looking out into the back yard full of green apples and figs, all the while stroking my fine blond hair.

Then one day Miss Ida just disappeared. Big Papa accused her of stealing fried apple pies off the stove. Come to find out, Granny had given her the pies. I never saw her again. She never came back. Did she wonder about me? Why didn't she walk the two blocks from her house to see if I was in the front yard?

My grandfather sat on the front porch with friends and complained about the first impression of the town that greeted visitors as they drove into Del City from Shreveport. Scattered on the hills above the highway were shanties, lean-tos, the Colored neighborhoods, right there in plain view, exposing the underbelly of the town.

There were rarely Colored people anywhere I was, except in the Jitney Jungle grocery store, even though our home was just one street over from their side of town.

If I walked by a Negro's house, I skipped fast. Often a dog, a fighting one, jumped off the porch, to growl and show his teeth. Then as I started to run, he came after me around some old car up on blocks in the front yard, to chase me away.

In the 1950s, African-American women were mostly relegated to working as maids in homes and often performed physically demanding work for very low wages. However, during this time, the widespread availability of appliances in the home left many domestic workers unemployed and they were forced to find work elsewhere.

Negroes, if they had jobs, worked for white men and depended on their generosity. Maids, like Ida, walked to work in white uniforms, garbage collectors balanced on the back of trucks, yardmen manicured around flowerbeds with a push mower. No blacks worked as mechanics, roughnecks in the oil fields or clerks in stores.

An exception was the black porter who hung out of the wide open doors as trains pulled into the station blasting a warning, one block from our house. I ran down the hill to watch them greet travelers and take their baggage. These porters were good-looking and immaculately dressed men: white shirts, starched collars, and white cuffs under dark navy blue jackets. The L&N logo fit between two skeins of gold braid on their flat navy caps.

When I heard that whistle blow, I flew down the gravel incline to wave and dream of taking a ride with a porter to carry my bags. I didn't know that at fourteen, Granny would finally let me ride all the way from Louisiana to Cincinnati in one of George Pullman's sleeper cars—to visit my mother for the first time.

After the Civil War, George Pullman, a railroad businessman, sought out employees to work on his development of the sleeper car. Prior to the 1860s, the concept of sleeper cars on railroads had not been widely popular.

The job of Pullman porter was one of the best a black man could aspire to, in status, and eventually pay. For 100 years, from the late 1860s until the late 1960s, Pullman was the biggest single employer of blacks in America.

The very nature of the job was a contradiction. The porter was servant as well as host. He had the best job in the community and the worst on the train.

Pullman knew there was a large pool of former slaves who would be looking for work after the Civil War and he had a clear racial concept. He was aware that most Americans, unlike the wealthy, did not have personal servants in their homes. Part of the appeal of traveling on sleeper cars, in a sense, was to experience an upper-class experience. Pullman was perceptive enough to realize that the men he hired already received the perfect training and "knew just how to take care of any whim that a customer had."

When train passengers called for a porter, who were by then fixtures on railroad cars, it became a custom to call all of them by the same name, "George" as if they were George Pullman's "boys," a practice that was begun in the South where slaves were named after their slave masters.

The only ones in the population to protest the custom were other men named George; hence, they founded the Society for the Prevention of Calling Sleeper Car Porters George or SPCSCPG. The group which claimed 31,000 members at one time, was more interested in defending the dignity of its white members than in achieving any measure of racial justice. Nevertheless, in 1926 the SPCSCPG persuaded the Pullman Company to install small racks in each car, displaying the name of the porter on duty. Of the 12,000 porters and waiters then working for Pullman, only 362 turned out to be named George.

Pullman porters are credited with a contribution to the development of the black middle class in America. In the late Nineteenth Century, they were among the only people in their communities to travel extensively. As a result, they became a conduit of new information and ideas from the wider world to their communities. Many Pullman porters saved rigorously in order to ensure that their children were able to obtain an education and better employment.

Thurgood Marshall, one of the lawyers who pleaded Brown v the Board of Education of Topeka before the Supreme Court, was a descendant of a Pullman porter.

Marshall knew that the Jim Crow system (*de jure* segregation) that separated the races in virtually all walks of southern life, in restaurants, hotels, theaters, waiting rooms, buses and trains, rest rooms, beaches, parks, cemeteries, even drinking fountains and telephone booths—was anchored on segregation in schools.

I graduated from segregated public schools in Del City in 1965 even though half of the population of the little North Louisiana town was African American. I don't remember knowing where the black school was located or thinking much about it.

I did not question 'Colored' water fountains, restrooms or why Negros must sit in the balcony in the movie theater—even when I was occasionally plummeted from above with ice and popcorn.

This was the life I knew.

As if the pressure of growing up in a small Southern town without my mother was not enough, I had to live up to my older sister's reputation. She knew everything about everything before I did. We got off to a particularly rough start when I arrived on her sixth birthday. She reminded me every ninth of July that she got no other presents that year. Just one sister.

Marilyn left for college first, to attend Louisiana Tech in Ruston. She decried the shabby neighborhoods in Del City. "There's no place for Coloreds to work in Del City, Donna. The young blacks will have to move to Atlanta or Chicago." When she came in from teacher training, she looked at the town through new eyes. "Donna, that's not right. Blacks have to use our old worn, outdated textbooks and their schools are broken down."

"I never thought about that." I was ashamed.

"You should think about it."

In 1961 when I went to Del City High School for the first time, Mrs. DeSordie's name was familiar. The home economics teacher was Marilyn's favorite.

Mrs. DeSordie called the role.

"Donna Fulmer."

"Here."

"Are you Marilyn Fulmer's sister?"

" Yes, Ma'am."

"Good. Great. What is Marilyn doing now?"

"She's in Arkansas. She's going to do graduate work in English at the University of Arkansas."

"I'm not surprised. She always made perfect bound button holes. Perfect. Do you like to sew?" she looked me in the eye.

"Not me. But I like to cook." I helped cook meals for the whole family since I was eleven.

With a pained look, she said, "We may get around to that."

We made green beans with almonds and homemade French dressing. That was it. We sewed the rest of the year.

When I made a 'C' in home economics, instead of an 'A' like my sister— when my pleats didn't lie down perfectly— Granny decided that the teacher must be getting too old to teach. I agreed.

The first time Marilyn came home after moving into the dormitory, I was puzzled by the way she spoke, "I go to Louieee seee ana Tech." she told Miss Altaline downtown at White's Dry Goods.

After we walked out, I said, "Marilyn, why were you talking so high falutin'? What's wrong with Loos'ana? You've only been gone a few weeks and you're already putting 'own' airs."

"The word 'on' is pronounced 'ahn' not 'own,' Donna."

"Are you too good for Del City now? Don't go to meddling," I shot back.

Later at the Purple Cow after having a hamburger, cherry coke, and BBQ potato chips to go, she scolded me, "Donna don't throw that sack of trash out of this car window, good grief! Pick up that paper right now and put it in the garbage can. We have to protect the environment. Someday the whole world will stink with sour, moldy liter."

"I am okay the way I am, Marilyn, thank you very much. Leave me alone!"

We rode past all the old houses on the hill coming into town on the Minden Road, giving rise to Marilyn's next monologue. "All of those houses need a good scrapping and a paint job. This town never changes. And children in the Negro schools use our old worn, outdated textbooks and their schools are broken down like these houses."

"You've told me that before." She was unaware that I could digest only so many challenges to my unexamined life at one sitting.

"You know, Donna, we've heard the 'n' word all our lives. I can't even say it. Daddy uses it, and his buddies, well, just about everybody. To choose teams we counted off with the rhyme, 'Eeny meeny miny, moe,' pointing to our next teammates. We didn't know any better, but now we do. Now you do. Donna. Don't ever use that word again. It's disrespectful."

"If somebody fixes Daddy's car poorly, he says it was n-----rigged. If a job outside was much harder than anticipated, he says he sweated like a...."

"Stop, Donna. That's what I mean. Don't ever say that word for *any r*eason!"

I sat quietly and thought about it. I knew my sister was right. Why does she always have to be so, so... right all the time? I wanted to please her more than anything in the world, to make her proud of me. I didn't want to be a slug.

"I've heard Daddy call people from South Louisiana 'coon asses,'" I said.

"Don't you understand that's offensive, contemptuous too? Do I have to tell you everything, Donna? You have so much to learn."

"What's contemptuous, Sis?"

"Think about the word," she said. "Break it down. Does *contemptuous* have a positive or a negative connotation?"

"Why do you trick me with one of your fifty cent words only to turn right around and use another one?" I snapped.

"We're home. I give up. Just forget about it, Donna. Get out of the car."

Except Marilyn never did forgot about it and continued to monitor my moral landscape, opening my eyes to the larger world. She kept the kudzu of prejudice and carelessness from taking root, taking hold in me, as I grew up in a small isolated Southern town.

When I became conscious of a society where inequality was routine, especially in schools, I felt the weight of an intense personal guilt. A teenager lying in bed at night, I thought, *I want to wake up to my surroundings and stop walking through life outright blindfolded.*

Part of the reason I was numbing out on life was that I was growing up with an alcoholic father. I was on duty for the family. I rarely did my homework, because—if there was not an immediate family crisis—there would be one soon. *If I worry about all the bad things that can happen, I will be prepared*. There was just so much emotional and physical energy, much of mine sucked out by fear. Marilyn coped with her fear by hiding in books. When I came in from school, I threw my books on the couch and ran outside until dark, never looking at them again until I picked them up the next morning. My schoolwork was not a priority for anyone, including me.

When it was time to go to college in 1965, I had determined not to become a teacher like my grandfather, my sister, my two aunts, my uncle and two cousins. Marilyn was already the gold standard, a Fulbright scholar.

Betty Endom American Airlines 1950s

Chapter 9
MUDDLING OUT INTO THE WORLD

My mother, a classical dancer, left Cincinnati when she was fourteen headed to New York with some homemade costumes to live with her sister and audition for some big shows. She finished the eighth grade and danced until she was twenty-nine.

My father, who was smart, but full of monkey business—perhaps already an alcoholic—quit school after the tenth grade and started working as a roustabout on an oil rig. His father never let him forget, "You didn't get your schoolin'."

I was raised not only by my paternal grandparents and my dad, but also by a collection of extended family who came and went routinely from our home. The circle of strong-willed educators began with my grandfather who got a two-year teaching certificate at the end of the 19th Century at a Normal Teacher's College in Huntsville, Texas. My Uncle Lemos was a professor at LSU, my aunt Mellie was a special education teacher, and my aunt Sugar refused to move from the 4th grade for forty years. Two of my first cousins were teachers, one a principal and my sister was getting a Master's Degree in English.

It would have been folly for me to say 'no' to all of these hangers-on, even though I was only a mediocre high school student. I was to follow my brother and sister into Louisiana Tech the summer after I graduated from Del City High School.

1965

My advisor at Louisiana Tech in Ruston, Louisiana, asked me, "What would you like to study?"

All she got was a vacant stare. "I don't know."

As she glanced over my high school grades with pursed lips, "Hmm..." She figured I didn't want to study much of anything.

To cheer her up I said, "In high school I majored in basketball and baton twirling."

But there was no charming her, and she suggested that I might consider a two-year secretarial course. "If you want to buckle down and work, there's nursing or maybe teaching."

"I don't want to be a teacher. How about airline stewardess?"

"Uh, we don't have that program. The airlines train their own employees. Here's a brochure. I think they prefer registered nurses. I hear that they fly to Havana, Cuba, from Key West, on gambling trips. I would not advise a nice young girl from the South to be a purser, a stewardess. Also, I believe young women have to sign an agreement to leave the job when they are about thirty-two years old. I'll tell you what, Miss Fulmer, you have a couple of days before registration to think about it. Let me know."

Airline stewardess. That would be an adventure. My next-door neighbor's daughter, Betty Endom, flies all over the world for American Airlines. I look at her when she comes home to visit, lounging in a sweat suit that looks freshly ironed. She has the perfect blond bubble hair, long red nails, narrow hips, and flawless skin with rosy cheeks.

I can get a nose job, the one where the surgeon turns around when he is almost done and pinches the sides with his fingertips to make it cute.

I am going to look at my assets for each job.

Qualifications: Female Flight Attendant at Eastern Airlines

1. 100 to 118 pounds no
2. Height 5 feet to 5 feet 4 inches no
3. Age 20 to 26 √
4. 20/40 vision no
5. High school graduate √
6. Single it all depends
7. The 'bloom' that goes with perfect health √

A few other competences might deem me unfit:

1. I have fine blond hair—sometimes green from chlorine—but always uncontrollable.

2. I bite my nails down to the quick and rip off my cuticles until they're red.
3. Not the right red.
4. I will have to glide effortlessly down that tiny isle. Then, without showing cleavage, bend over to find a man's ear and whisper in a breathy tone, so as not to disturb his neighbor, "Now what can I get for you, sir?"

Nursing. I am not considering this one. I got plenty of bedpan experience when I slept with my grandmother until she died. I adored my grandmother but I do not want to get up during the night to do the potty thing for somebody else's granny.

Secretary. I am too global. That is to say, I have failed at that already. I landed a summer job two years ago typing letters for Brother Hall, my Baptist minister. I changed his wording around if I thought my writing improved his communication. A couple of times when I addressed letters to major contributors to the building fund, I misspelled their name on the envelope— just one letter off. Nobody is perfect.

What is left? I am back to teaching. However, I am not sure I even like kids. What do I like to do? I like to play basketball. Physical Education teacher, that's it. That would be far enough away from Marilyn's English major and Jane Austen.

When I finished my education degree and had my first class at Renville High School, I answered my own question; I did like kids. They made me laugh about something every day. Like when Gay Nell raced down the basketball court only to make a goal for the opponent, I bent over and let out my big guttural laugh. It was a sound from deep down, an animal noise, the Fulmer roar. The students gave me a quizzical look and could not figure out what animal.

I was especially drawn to students who were a little rough around the edges. Asia, my P.E. assistant, was a black student who lived with her grandparents, had no cardigan on cool mornings (that's extra), and an alcoholic father.

Maybe I was doing what Eric Berne in TA (transactional analysis) suggested, reparenting the child's ego state. Nevertheless, kids were fun and funny and school was a natural place for me, steered there by my family lineage.

The First Baptist Church in Del City was also part of my extended family. I was in church three times a week: Sunday school and worship service where I sang in the choir, Training Union and more preaching Sunday night with youth fellowship afterward, and then Girl's Auxiliary on Wednesday, choir practice, and more preaching. An archetype of goodness, I figured I was left behind at the starting gate, having the roughneck for a father.

He came in drunk one afternoon and I showed up at the church crying. My youth director, Michael, invited me to go over and spend the afternoon with his young wife, Shelly. I could tell she was moving in and did not expect a visitor, but she came to the door and invited me in. I had cookies and milk and helped her fold clothes. She taught me the secret of folding a fitted sheet. We didn't have fitted sheets at my house—that was extra—but I made notes in my head, to be used over and over again in the years after I left home. Her slightly overweight body, sweet smile and thick brown hair comes to mind when I look down in a clothesbasket and pull up a fitted sheet.

1968

When I was in college, I had a strong spiritual yearning to go into full-time church ministry of some kind. I became president of the Baptist Student Center in the spring of my junior year in college and applied to be a summer missionary during the summer break. I filled out the application, got recommendations, and went for an interview in New Orleans. And waited.

The college post office was a repetitious oil painting, hundreds of small gold mailboxes, long rows side to side, up and down—a puzzle to find the right one. Weeks after I sent in my application, I turned the tiny key in my mailbox, 559 in the middle of row 46. I was excited when I saw a return address on an envelope, the one I had been looking for, the one that could change my life—or not—for the summer: Home Mission Board,

Southern Baptist Convention, 1350 Spring St., N.W., Atlanta, Georgia 30309.

I have to get somewhere alone to open this. It feels like a one pager, probably a rejection, "We regret to inform you..." I found a bench and sat down before I ripped open the envelope and started reading:

Assignment Sheet

Name Donna Gwyn Fulmer

You have been assigned to HAWAII to serve under the general direction of Mr. Malcolm Stuart, 1225 Nehoa Street, Honolulu, Hawaii 96822 who will be advising you concerning place and date you are to report.

You will find enclosed a card to be signed and returned immediately in acceptance of the assignment.

Note: Inquire of the above named supervisor if you desire additional information concerning the nature of your work, or the type of clothing and materials you should bring.

3/68

I could not move. Glorietta, New Mexico, a church camp, was as far as I had ever traveled from home. I thought I would yell, or laugh or cry if I got good news, but I sat quietly, numb with disbelief.

As the days unfolded, I learned that I would be living on four of the Islands during the summer: Oahu, Maui,

Kauai, and Molokai; staying with local host families from the churches.

This would be my chance for an adventure but also a chance to clear my mind and decide if I wanted to marry Max, the man I was engaged to. *Yes, this will be a perfect time to get away.*

I would be one of thirteen college students assigned to the Hawaiian Islands. We would teach Bible school, organize programs, give talks, and support the small Baptist missions in any way we could. When we came home, we would visit churches and present slide presentations of the Islands that would lead to a discussion with congregations about our mission work in the assigned areas.

When I changed planes in San Francisco to go to Oahu, I was surprised to see a familiar face, Leslie, from the Baptist Student Center—in uniform!

I ran to him, "Why are you in uniform? Did you sign up? Were you drafted? You'd be the last person I would think of ... would think would...be a soldier."

When I finally let him say something, Leslie said he flunked out of school and signed up for the army. He was headed to Vietnam after basic training. I picked up his cap and flopped down in the seat next to him hoping I could stay. I couldn't breathe. I touched him, held his hand, put my arm around his neck to feel the starched shoulders, and looked down at the thick lace-up boots. Suddenly I put on his cap to be silly, but mostly to see if this could be real. Leslie was a gentle guy with a huge heart. *I hope they put him in the typing pool. I can't see him firing a gun.*

"Excuse me, Miss, that's my seat." I looked up at the stranger holding his bag.

"I got to go to my seat. Give me a hug. I love you. Oh, Leslie, take care of yourself. Watch out over there, watch out and take care of yourself... Uh, come to see me if you get R&R back home."

"I will," he said, "I love you too, Donna. Here's my address. Write to me."

"Sure. I will. I promise."

I know why my grandmother and her friends often referred to loose women. I felt I was let loose for the first time in my life, in Hawaii.

Handsome, spontaneous dark-skinned men and women greeted me at the airport in the "aloha spirit" with pineapple juice and white plumeria leis, wearing their brilliantly flowered, relaxed clothing. They expressed the laid-back and nature-loving culture of the Islands that instantly soaked into my bones.

I stood to wait for my group at an outdoor market, an otherworldly image of bounteous baskets: yellow-orange papayas, thick red guava juice, purple cymbidium orchids and gold spiky pineapples.

I was also a ripened fruit, overdue with possibilities, soon to be sashaying in a glowing pink muu muu, white flowers and green leaves, punctuated with a dark tan.

Carol and I were partners going from home to home and church to church. Our first assignment was the Pearl

City Church, nestled in the hills over Waikiki Beach. Richard and Betty Sakata, a Japanese family, would be our hosts for three weeks.

Nineva Tupua was Samoan, tall, dark, and enormous. He was a convert to the Baptist faith and a member of the Pearl City Church. He taught Bible school with Carol and me, always helpful bringing the ice and refreshments to our beautiful Chinese, Japanese, Hawaiian, and Haole (Caucasian) children. Nineva showed up wherever we were and even drove us to services in the evenings. Carol and I were together with him singing, planning, eating, learning about the Islands and generally having fun. The Sakatas made him our unofficial tour guide.

At night, I lay in bed and smelled the ocean from my bedroom window before I nodded off to the rise and fall of the waves. Only a few months ago, such an experience was offered to me only in the movies. I whispered a prayer of graditude.

That first weekend on Oahu, we went to Waikiki Beach and watched Nineva take a shovel and stuff hot coals in a pig's belly, then throw him in a deep hole, Kalua pig, for a teen bonfire the next night. As we took a walk back to the car, I screamed when one of the many tiny frogs jumped out of the grass onto my feet. The next time I jumped, Nineva grabbed my hand and did not let go. Carol looked at me. A romance would be frowned upon. *I hope I can trust Carol.*

Nineva and I found ourselves holding hands whenever we could. It was magical.

When we were finally alone in the car one night, I couldn't resist. I reached up and we kissed. He was bewitching. His wiry black hair felt mysterious to my fingertips. I was falling in love. The Island had me under its spell.

We managed to stay in touch as I did my swing through the other Islands that summer. I knew I would see him in Oahu, because we would all gather there before we went home.

While I was away, when I lay down one night to listen to the waves, I started thinking, *what would happen if I stayed*? Nineva could become a minister and I would be the minister's wife, missionaries together. *What if I decided not to go home*? I would never have to tell Max anything. I would simply disappear; never go home.

When I got back to Oahu, but before I could tell Nineva about my plan, he gave me a big kiss, then held my shoulders back and took a long look at me, "Don't wear so much white makeup, Donna. You've got a nice tan."

"Okay." *I don't think I have on makeup. What is he trying to say to me? Doesn't he realize I am a haole? That birthmark is a hard one to miss*. His eye-opening revelation sneaked out.

I was shaken. Apprehension was an interloper in my script that had a happy ending.

One not to be dissuaded easily, I went headlong, and popped the question, "Nineva, what if I stayed. Could we get married?"

He began to name the aunts, uncles and cousins he was to bring over from Samoa, who would live with us. “I’ve been saving for years, Donna. The whole family will be coming.”

I gathered with the other students at the airport with my airline ticket in hand.

When I kissed Nineva good-bye, we both knew we would never see each other again.

I paused to take my last long look at the water, the Ocean I had come to reverence, the translucent blue that to this day I cede only to those Islands.

Sobbing on the plane, I thought, *how could I love Max and so readily fall in love with Nineva?*

My feelings about marriage moved back and forth from ambivalence to out and out stark fear when I got back home. Max never knew about Nineva Tupua.

Leslie did not make it back from the war. I never wrote like I promised.

Because these are class actions, because of the wide applicability of this decision, and because of the great variety of local conditions, the formulation of decrees in these cases presents problems of considerable complexity. On reargument, the consideration of appropriate relief was necessarily subordinated to the primary question—the constitutionality of segregation in public education.

BROWN V. BOARD OF EDUCATION 1954

Chapter 10

WOMMAN WEL AT EASE

1980

When I stepped into a woman's conference in Mobile, I walked toward a prominent art exhibit, a three quarter portrait in shadow of a woman's face with a strong jaw. As I got closer, I saw the words below and recognized the Middle English. *Interesting.* "I am myne owene womman wel at ease."

It has been a struggle. My singular plan was to become 'at ease' and stop overcompensating for insecurity by sucking all of the air out of a room when I walked in. The clothes I was wearing, an African dashiki and Birkenstocks, was a beginning.

Max and I did marry and when he got out of the army, we settled in Mobile, Alabama, and I continued to teach P.E.

I found myself pregnant with my second boy, due in May. Perfect. I could work almost an entire year. My principal did not see it that way. He was not happy with a pregnant P.E. teacher who could not coach softball that spring. When I came back in the fall, I was punished with an involuntary transfer to LaFleet High School, a larger inner city school.

It was shocking that the principal was transferring me after six years. "He has obviously made a deal with the other principal so I have nothing to say about it," I cried and fussed to Max.

Going to a new school was not like my first job, but close to it. Each school has a particular culture that you must figure out—and adjust to—in order to be successful.

I knew there was a committed and dedicated staff at LaFleet, but because of its location, there was also the possibility of off-campus disturbances. *My job just got harder.*

The LaFleet school building was past its prime but it stood in the heart of the city like a self-respecting old man, full of pride, with gleaming white wainscoting and sparkling halls.

A senior English literature class was assigned to me along with my Physical Education classes at the new school. I had mostly boys for fifth period Lit, right before they went out for football practice, the last period of the day.

Entering my English class the first day, I looked around and saw a room full of men folded into desks made for boys. *Okay. Don't panic.*

The senior English curriculum began with the Old English poem, *Beowulf* and Chaucer's, *The Canterbury Tales.*

How can I engage this class in early literature when it is so difficult for me to relate to?

To introduce Chaucer and *Beowulf,* I thought of my piece of art. A visual might help them see how Middle English evolved into something we can read.

I held up the shadow portrait I bought at the woman's conference. "What do you see?"

"I see a woman's face, kind of." Alphonse said with a broom straw hanging out of his mouth. He was stretched out with his feet under the desk in front of him, arms crossed.

"Good Alphonse, it is the silhouette of a woman's face—and take that broom straw out of your mouth, please. Do you think she is a strong woman or a bashful woman, class?"

"Strong, look at that chin."

"Right. Ricky. She has a strong, square jaw doesn't she?"

"Okay, who has figured out the words at the bottom?"

"Katie said, why is it written so crazy? I am mine—something—woman. That's all I can make out."

"Can anybody help her out?"

"Okay, Alphonse, do you have it?"

He kicked the girl's desk in front of him with glee. "I got it! I am mine woman well at ease. I can't get that 'owene' word."

"Great. Here it is: 'I am mine own woman well at ease.'

"Now what does that mean?" I asked. "If you are at ease are you uptight or relaxed?"

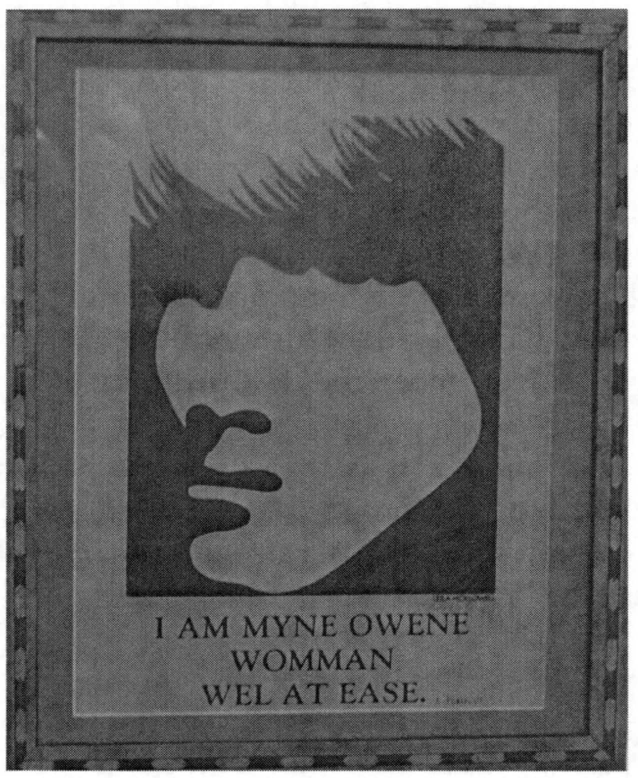

"I'll be relaxed when I get a smoke." Alphonse tapped the girl's shoulder beside him and made her tee-hee. Then she waved him off. *There is an Alponse in every class who sucks out the air.*

Katie said, "It means she's relaxed and she don't need no man."

"Yes, Katie, she's telling us how she feels about herself, but it isn't about a man, is it? She may have a husband or boyfriend. We don't know, do we? Does anyone have an idea why these words are so difficult to read?"

"These are words from back in the old days," Janice said.

"Yes, quite a while back. The reason that these words are difficult to read is that they were written in Old English. Then they were translated into Middle English because Old English would be like a foreign language to us. We couldn't have guessed the caption on the picture at all. In graduate school, I had to gain fluency in reading Middle English.

Have you ever thought of how difficult it is for a Mexican student to learn English? Can you think of a word in English that is pronounced the same, but is spelled differently and has a different meaning? There are lots of them, aren't there?"

"Bare and bear, b- a- r- e and b- e- a- r." Joyce stopped yacking to her neighbor for a minute to blurt out an answer.

"Good, Joyce—I didn't know you were with me. Our language is a borrowed language from several Germanic tribes in the eleventh century, the Angles, Saxons, Frisii and Jutes (Danes). Our language dates back to 1066, the year that they were conquered by the Normans who were French. What century are we in now?"

Jackie answered from the back, "the Nineteenth Century, it's 1980."

"Everybody knows that," Kathy said. "It's the Twentieth Century, dumb boy!"

"This is what I'm getting at. The Century is one number larger than the actual year. When we get to the Twenty-first Century, what years will we be in?"

"Twenty something," they answered together.

"If our language evolved into English from the Saxons and Jutes in the Eleventh Century, what year would it have been? I just told you."

"Ten something, they answered.

"Write this down. It will be on the test. Someone came up with 1066 as the date for the beginning of the English language. Because there were no printing presses to copy this new Germanic language, the first authors and the dates on the writing were sometime lost. That's the case with Beowulf, the long narrative poem we are going to read. We don't know the author of Beowulf and we don't know exactly when it was written, somewhere between the Eighth Century and the early Eleventh Century. Now some of you guys get in on the discussion. Glen, can you can remember being afraid of monsters?" I asked the shy student on the front row.

"I'm afraid of monsters—those real ones—who hide down under the steering wheel when they drive by real slow in a caddie." Alphonse blurted out with the straw in his mouth again. *I'll ignore it for now.*

"Alphonse, see me after class, please. What is a caddie?"

"One of those long, low to the ground Cadillacs"

"Okay, I was referring to some of the monsters in your children's books. Ah, well, let's move on. *Beowulf* will not be that difficult even though the language sounds strange. There are good guys and bad guys. Got it? We will read most of it together. Or some days you will get with a neighbor and figure it out in pairs."

"Turn to *Beowulf* on page ten of your text." I waited until they stopped flipping pages. "Beowulf is the Prince of the Geats from Sweden. He is our hero. The villain is Grendel the monster and...There's the bell. We will continue with the introduction tom...

Sit down students. I am not finished. Try to read some of *Beowulf* tonight and tell me something about the story tomorrow. Okay? Stop. Come back and sit down." I waved the students away from the door. "You are dismissed on my voice, not on the bell. You do not jump up while I am talking." *I hear groans.* "Now everyone is seated. You are dismissed."

Alphonse stayed behind, came up front, and plopped down on the edge of my desk.

I began, "Alponse, I have a sense of humor. I think I am pretty easy to get along with. But, I do not play. When I walked down the aisle by your desk, you pulled on my skirt. That will not happen again. Do you want to graduate?"

"Hey, Miss, don't get so excited. I'm sorry." He put his hands over his face. "You gonna have a heart attack if you get upset over a little something like that. Yes, Miss, Miss, you better loosen up a little. It'll be alright."

He's not comfortable trying to pronounce my name. "Mrs. Orchard. My name is Orchard, like the apple orchard, Alphonse. And take that straw out of your mouth.

"Okay, Miss 'O'. Chill. I'll see you tomorrow," and he ran out.

Gee.

We dressed out for the first time in P.E. the next day. I was enthusiastic at the first class on this new assignment with the squad lines drawn out on my clipboard.

"Where is the equipment?" I asked Mrs. Dumas, head of the department. I figured out quickly that as a new teacher, my class would be assigned outside, very few days inside in the gym.

"There's three basketballs in that bag, she said. We use the old ones outside. One is flat. You can get the needle fro..."

"No, that's okay. It's time to line them up for roll call. I have the junior and senior boys first period."

"Mrs.Orchard, you'll do okay. Just let them play a little bit and break up the fights if they get too bad." *Mrs. Dumas' attempt at encouragement.*

"I gotcha..." *if it gets too bad.*

I recognized some of the seniors from my English class. I'm not sure they can imagine their English teacher in a pair of shorts—ever. When I walked onto the depleted, thirsty outdoor basketball court I noticed—no net on the rim.

I was aware of being self-conscious; *I should get knee length shorts. These Bermuda's look more like short shorts. Imagine this 'cracker' teaching these tall guys basketball. There is something ironic here. I had better keep my sense of humor.*

I am a tall woman, five feet ten inches; however, I was dwarfed as they circled around me. *I can't act intimidated.* I saw Alphonse from English class and ran up to him to say, “Hi,” but he looked away. I thought he might help me.

The P.E. schedule was basic. In my plan book, it was written “basketball and volleyball when we are inside the gym.” The secret: It was always *basketball*. If we were outside, the official plan was “basketball or baseball”—*basketball again.* Basketball skills all year were completely compatible with my survival skills.

I heard mumbling coming from a group of students, “Fellas looka here. Oh, yeah. Ah huh, My. My. My. Oh, man. Looka here. I’m gonna like this class.”

“Shut up, Kedrick, and leave the lady alone,” Alphonse stepped up.

“First we’re going to line up in squads and I’ll call the roll. Okay, alphabetical order, six to a row.”

“What’s your name Miss?”

“We’ll get to that, just listen for your name. Cedric, Lydell, Kendrick, Alphonse, Fred… Good. My name is Mrs. Orchard, gentlemen, and we will all get along. I came from Newman High. Now I know all of you can play basketball, but we will have structure, be orderly about it: line up in your squads every morning, choose teams…Got it?”

“Give me a ball, Miss.” Lydell said.

“Wait, I get the first shot.” I said.

“She made it!” somebody yelled. “That was a short one. Bet she can’t hit one from behind this circle,” Alphose got a stick and started keeping score in the sand. “Ha, you missed!” They were tickled.

"Hey give me another try on the long shot"—woosh in the goal! "Take that gentlemen." *I was lucky.*

"Get outa here. That lady can shoot," somebody in the front squad nodded.

"Here's the ball, guys."

"We'll be good, Miss. I'm Donald. I was the other P.E. teacher's official assistant." He was short, a little overweight with beautiful blue eyes. Donald was not chosen for a team.

"Thanks, Donald. You can help me with the names until I get to know everybody."

"Jerry already gave you a fake name. Didn't you hear everybody laugh? Over there, that's Ronald Jenkins. You don't have to worry about him too much. He has a job on the street. You won't see him on Friday cause that's when his people got money. On Monday…"

"Ah. I see."

"Did you have to go to school to be a P.E. teacher, Miss Orchard?"

"Well, of course, Donald. I have a college degree like the rest of the teachers. At the last school, I had a whole program set up. We had lots of equipment there. Well, yeah, P.E. is more than just throwing a ball out there. I would like to teach some lifetime sports, activities that you could play after you graduate. I am the tennis coach here at LaFleet too. Are you interested in tennis?"

"I don't know about that. There haven't been any nets on the tennis court since I been here, the last three years. Finally they put up two more basketball goals on the tennis court." Donald said.

"No nets? What?" I raised my eyebrow.

"Ain't nobody playing tennis anyway." Donald must have figured that ended the idea of a tennis team.

"No one at this school plays tennis." I corrected Donald's English.

"I just told you that," he said.

"Well, Donald, we are going to get nets on there. You can be the tennis team manager. Whatcha think? Mr. Weaver told me I could coach a tennis team, organize to play the other high schools in the county. I'm all excited about it."

"Skate boarding is my thing."

"Gotcha, Dona..."

Pop. Pop. Pop. Pop.

"Who has a cap pistol?" When I wheeled my body around toward the noise, the scene was suddenly in slow motion while an inertia kept my feet planted. As the dust cleared, I could see that I was the only person standing.

"Hit the dirt, Miss Orch, it's a piece, a drive-by across the street at the U-Carry!" Alphonse reached over and pulled me to the ground with his big outstretched hand.

I could taste the dust and dirt as my knees were thump, thump, thumping on the ground.

It got quiet. *I'm not sure my legs will hold me up.*

"I hear the boys coming. We can start playing again. Get on up, Miss" Alphonse said. "They won't be back."

"What do you mean? You cannot start playing! They might come back around. The cashier is still hiding inside."

I called all the students over to me. "Is anybody hurt?"

Kedrick said, "We're all okay, Miss."

"You all have to sit on these benches next to me. Sit down. Let's talk about this. I want to look at you to see that everybody's okay. If you saw anything and can fill out a witness report, see me after class." *I'm glad I thought about that. On Dragnet, they always said the first twenty-four hours after an incident is critical. They don't even know who Joe Friday is.*

I heard the sirens coming down the street, then three police cruisers pulled up on the curb outside the U-Carry.

"Throw me that ball," Alphonse said. "Next time you see a Caddie cruisin' real slow, Miss O, everybody in the car leaning—hit the ground. You'll be okay."

We used to call the police the 'fuzz' and in the 60s, 'pigs.' I am glad to see them today.

"Donald, run up to the office and get Mr. Weaver. Quick, honey. Okay, you guys still have a few minutes to play," I said. "I'm going to sit down over here under this tree." I started my breathing. *Breath in the good…ten; blow out the bad…ten.*

"Are you okay, Miss Orchard. You don't look so good." Donald looked me in the eye when he got back from the office. "Mr. Weaver said he would be out here in a few minutes. I told him nobody was hurt."

"I'm okay. Watch things for me a minute, Donald." I continued the breathing.

When I got to my English class fifth period, Jackie said, "I heard you had to hit the ground, Miss Orchard. What happened?"

Ignoring his comment, "Okay, I have twenty-nine of you seniors in here and we have work to do."

"We all go to football next period, Miss. We get hyped up,"

"I am aware of that, Ronald, but this is English fifth period." I held up the text, "Do you see how thick this English literature book is? We have to cover the whole thing so you can pass the school test, the county test, the state test and my final exam in here. If you do well, I will make lots more money. That was a joke guys."

"Then you could get some better clothes."

"Yes, Alphonse, you have a point." We all laughed.

"How many of you tried to read *Beowulf* on your own?" No hands went up.

Katie said, "I was going to, but I forgot."

"I like you Miss Orch."

"I like you too, Alphonse. Oh, well, follow along and I'll read the introduction to *Beowulf*..."

"Aw, Miss Orch, this ain't a real monster. This thing is too long. This is not like the monsters in the hood."

"The bell is about to ring. I am going to rest a minute. You read the first part where the monster kills the people in Heorot, in the dining hall. That's your homework. Be prepared for a discussion."

"You sit down. You don't look so good. We'll be alright. I'll take care of these 'chillens' for ya."

"Thanks, Alphonse."

There's the bell.

"You get some rest. We're mostly going to get into college if we can play football or basketball. We goin' to take care of it. Just chill."

"Bye Alphonse. Go."

Is my daddy a monster?

Portable Building in Grand Bay, Alabama

Chapter 11

PARKER MIDDLE SCHOOL 1992

Mobile, Alabama

I was prepared when I walked into Parker Middle School with the proper mahogany nameplate, somewhat dusty, designed years ago for each of the jobs I missed out on: Donna F. Orchard, Assistant Principal.

The building was a pleasant contemporary brick, glassed in foyer. In the front hall, I recognized that smile, an old pal from Grider Middle.

"I'm happy to see a familiar face, Katie. You look great. Never age with that beautiful skin."

"Thanks, Donna. But believe me I'm not as young as we were way back when. What ya doing over here?"

"I'm the new assistant principal."

"Get out of here! I didn't know you wanted to be a principal. ...Sure you want this job over here, girlfriend? Oh, we'll all help you. That'll be great. How is your son, the one born about the same time Sam was born?"

"He's at McGill. Loves it. Max pays the tuition. Oh, we were divorced in 1982, but he's the best father, the best. I'll give you the details later. I've been applying for every open position for three or four years. Tired of knocking on doors. I'm going to let myself have five minutes of *ata boys.*"

"Come here, Donna. I've got to whisper this. I don't want Agnes at the front desk to hear. Billy Black said he hired the woman who had the best legs to be his assistant. He didn't tell us who it was. Can you believe—that Bubba? Don't worry about it. Just wanted you to know. He's got a reputation."

"What? Are you serious? He's definitely—Billy Bob." Laughing. "Eat your heart out. He barely comes up to my shoulders. Got to go. We'll catch up later. Hey, Katie, watch my back, girl."

"You know it."

The door was open: Principal, Billy Black.

" Hi Mr. Black. Do you have a minute?"

"Sure. Hi, Donna. Looks like we both made it out of our portables in Grand Bay."

"Remember when we hit the lucky number of 104 degrees?" I chimed in. "We walked our middle schoolers to the gym for their safety—no air conditioning there either—to sit for the rest of the day to sweat it out with 500 kids. I never understood why Mr. Sawyer wouldn't let us buy a window unit with our own money—it wouldn't be fair unless every portable had one—all the while sitting in his air conditioned office."

"We do have air conditioning here," Mr. Black said, "but there are other problems with this modern building with low ceilings. Let me show you around. This school has an open plan, an experimental design—a failed experiment. It's all open around a big circle. You see." He pointed to the first classroom, "No doors at the entrances of the rooms and few windows. Teachers complain that the building makes them sick, literally ill."

"How so?" My mental picture of a comfortable environment was fading fast.

"You can't get fresh air in here because most of the rooms don't have windows, and if they do, the windows are sealed shut because of the air conditioning. This carpet covers the whole building except the cafeteria, bathrooms, stage and gym. I had a teacher take a leave of absence because of respiratory problems she attributed to the building. With over 1200 students, you can't keep the carpet clean."

I looked around the corner at miles of carpet, all dirty blue. I cannot get away from that color.

"What's under here? Could you tile it?" I tried to be helpful.

"Yes, I've got the work order in," he said, "but who knows when they'll get to it. I want all this damn carpet pulled up and tile the whole thing, the library too."

As we walked down the hall by the library, I saw a lanky boy running through the stacks. Mr. Black obviously didn't see him.

I thought out loud, "The architect of this building sure failed to understand middle schoolers. Can't a student in one class rock back in her chair on the back row and see into this neighboring room, even make signs or talk to somebody in this next class?"

"Exactly," he continued. "Most of the teachers drag book cases or anything they can find to construct a barricade, a wall of any kind to avoid the noise and traffic."

I moved a pushcart to enter the classroom "I see that most of them have pushed these carts or tables together to fabricate an entrance." *Teachers are tremendously resourceful. That's a diplomatic way to say we are expected to turn out an excellent product all the while using both feet to kick the obstacles out of the way.*

"Right." Mr. Black began to describe a new plan. "Now all the students move from one class to another, on the same bell around this huge circle. It's a mess. Too many fights and confusion. You and I will train the faculty this year in the new model middle school program. We will divide the students into small groups under the guidance of a core group of teachers, across disciplines, who will then act as advisors and mentors."

My head started to feel fuzzy right before my eyes glazed over—I checked out of the present company—emotional overload. *I hope he doesn't notice.*

"The idea is: no bells. The students move at different times in student teams with their team teachers. Twelve hundred middle schoolers moving around in this big circle at one time doesn't work. We have a tough time being everywhere: in the halls, in the bathrooms, at the lockers, and I only have you and Mr. Bruse. You'll meet him. He's worthless. Walks around dressed in a suit doing nothing. Trying to look important. I'll show you where your office is. Go ahead and look around. I've got to go to a school board meeting. Write down your questions. We'll meet tomorrow. Glad you're here and I'll have some help."

The same tall boy that was in the library peeked around the corner at us, then ran.

I walked into my roomy office, no dirty blue walls. My nameplate looked professional on the front of the glass-topped desk. I forgot to bring my blue blazer to hang on the coat rack. I should keep one in the office in case I have to go in front of a camera to make a statement. My administrator friend told me I will always look like a principal if I put a dark navy blazer over whatever I am wearing that day—and check for cleavage. I will try not to make statements to the press and I definitely want to keep the school off the front page. Sex and money are the two fast tracks to the headlines.

I sat back in my fake leather chair and felt myself relax, until I remembered: I don't know what the hell I'm doing. I'm shocked at Mr. Black's disrespect for the other assistant principal. I wonder what errors in judgement will expose me as an imposter—to be thrown down into Mr. Black's chute, flipping over and over, clunk, clunk, clunk, finally landing at the bottom with a dull thud to sit by Mr. Bruse—worthless.

There was no orientation or internship for assistant principals, just a letter telling me to report to Parker Middle School. Sure, I got certified for administration. Yes, I went to school for this. Guess I forgot to take notes that day: large urban middle schools with no doors to the classrooms or windows.

I can use the phone and go to the bathroom anytime I wish. Hello real world! Assistant Principal on my door. Can't you just enjoy the moment, Donna?

I have heard that this is a rough school, but I could not ask Mr. Black about that. It might have killed my chances right there. A woman cannot acknowledge any fear. If she does, she is a wimp. If she is assertive, she is a bitch. *There is a fine line we walk, sisters.*

My plan after I finished this last degree: I will become a beloved principal until I am eighty, the principal of history, of memory; the one everyone refers to years later as "back in the good old days."

Intuition intruded. Reality lies somewhere between my own segregated public school experience and the idealistic myths I learned about public schools at the University.

I thought of something. Mr. Black is white and Mr. Bruse is black. When Mr. Black was a coach, he used the 'N' word if he felt like it. I was shocked. I used to think in Renville on my first job. "Is everything about race?" Secretly, from the boardroom to the coffee pot, yes, everything in public schools is about race.

We were eighty percent black at Parker, low income. I transferred from a predominately-white school, low income, at Grand Bay. Many of these children in both schools needed a variety of services from the school and community outside the classroom. I spent much of my time as an assistant principal acting as a conduit—talking with overworked counselors, social workers, case workers, special education teachers and tired parents who worked two or three jobs—to get children the help that they needed.

Mr. Black picked up the paddle on his desk and proudly raised it in the air, wooden with a dark patina. I figured if I wanted to teach students not to hit each other, I should not hit them. I'd just strangle them.

About middle schoolers. I did take notes that day. They can be a dangerous population. They will bring a knife or gun to school to scare a bully, to level the playing field. High schoolers are generally mature enough to consider the consequences.

Two Days Later

"Mr. Black, why does that tall boy, all arms and legs, run around in the hall during the day? He doesn't seem to be in anyone's class."

"Oh, that's just Josie. He's crazy."

The next time I saw Josie stealthily peeking around the corner, I decided to catch him. "Hi, I'm Mrs. Orchard, the new assistant principal. I'd like to shake your hand. What is your name?"

"Josie J. Johnson. Who are you?"

"I'll be around here every day. Come with me and we'll see where you're supposed to be third period."

"I'm not going. Can I see your room?"

"Ah, I'll show you around my office if you'd like and then you'll have to go to Miss Wright's class. I'll walk you over there."

I almost tripped over Josie when he slipped past me as I unlocked the office door. "You got lots of stuff in here. Can I staple?" He picked up the stapler from my desk.

"Oh, I have an appointment at 10:00 o'clock, but sure, I'll let you come in and help me sometime. Come on, let's go down the hall."

When we got to the classroom, his teacher looked up surprised, "Mrs. Wright, I found Josie missing in action again."

"Oh, thank you, Mrs. Orchard. When you have time, we need to set up another IEP (Individualized Education Plan) meeting with Josie's grandmother, if we can get in touch with her."

"I'll get in touch with her and set up a meeting. I'll let you know. It will have to be after school for me."

"Okay."

Before my appointment, I searched through a stack of NMSA (National Middle School Association) Journals still on the floor. I was sure that one featured FAS (fetal alcohol syndrome) recently; *yes, here it is, May 1991*. I flipped through the article. I had seen these characteristics before. Josie had small, widely spaced eyes, flat midface, poor impulse control, loss of IQ points...

Agnes buzzed. "Mrs. Trimble is here, Mrs. Orchard."

"Thank you, Agnes. Send her in."

Agnes, at the front desk, was a short, overweight black woman who had her own style. She wore some bling every day, either a heavy necklace or a colorful designer scarf. She had been the personal secretary for many principals over the years. The "go to" person at the school, she was professional, kind, and efficient; had my back when an angry parent came into the building.

"Come in Mrs. Trimble. I am Mrs. Orchard. I'm glad you got my message. Have a seat."

"Is something wrong?"

"As I explained on your answering machine, I want to prevent problems. Danielle had good grades at Parker until eighth grade. Her science teacher pulled up her seventh grade report card and found that she had mostly 'As' and 'Bs' last year. Here is her first quarter report card this year. She is failing science, math and P.E. P.E., of all things. She must not be dressing out. Also, she's missed eleven days since school started. I would like to see her bring those grades up and get ready for high school next year. She can clearly do the work."

The mother leaned forward, "She's had stomach problems this week, her time of the month, you know. But she's here today."

"Good. She was out three days last week and the week be..." The door flew open. I looked up. "Josie, what are you doing opening my door? I'm in a conference."

"I love you Miss O, I love you Miss O."

"Go on Josie. Did you hear me? Go back to class. I'm going to close this door now. Take your foot out of the door. This is my office, Josie. Take your foot out of this door, now! Excuse me, Mrs. Trimble. I'm terribly sorry."

"I understand."

I buzzed, "Mr. Black, uh, Josie has interrupted my conference and he, well, he won't take his foot out of my door. Can you come over here and get him?"

Mr. Black looked around the door, "He's gone now, Mrs. Orchard. If he comes back, call and have him picked up. We can't get anybody at home. Their phone is disconnected."

"Are you serious? Have him picked up? Call the police?"

"Yeah, maybe they'll eventually send him to Mt. Miegs. He's got a long arrest record."

"Sorry, Mrs. Trimble. Hold on another minute. We will get Danielle in here and talk to her. I'll call Mrs. Mitchell's room. She's in social studies. "

When the door was slung open wide, it was not Danielle, but Josie. Let me think...Let me think...

"Sit right here in the back, Josie. I'll give you some paper and these colored pencils. I need some artwork for my bare walls. Is your grandmother home today?"

"What is your favorite color, Miss O?" he asked.

"Just anything."

Danielle walked in.

"You're just going to have to get up in the morning, Danielle." Her mother started in on her. "You know I have to be at work at five a.m. I'm the morning manager." She looked at me, "at the Waffle House in Theodore."

"Yes Ma'am."

"You have to catch that bus at 7:15. They won't wait on you, baby."

"Yes Ma'am."

"Mrs. Trimble, maybe you could call Danielle and wake her up at six o'clock, make sure she's up and dressed? Could you take a break?"

"We aren't allowed to use the phone at work." she said.

"Do you have a break in the mornings?" I probed.

"My break isn't until nine o'clock."

"Tell you what. I have a suggestion. Maybe your boss will let you take that break early, at six, so you can call Danielle and wake her up. Danielle, do you think that will work?"

"Mrs. Orchard, line two. It's the Central Office."

"Thank you, Agnes. Excuse me, Mrs. Trimble. I have to take this. Yes. Yes. I have a TB test on record. Yes, I'm at Parker Middle now. Yes, Assistant Principal. Taxes? Just leave my deductions the same. Yes, ma'am."

"Look Miss O. This is a picture of my blue book bag, Josie holds up his picture from the back of the room. Can you see these dots? That's the zipper."

"Nice. Now I'm busy. Why don't you go to see if Mrs. Wright is looking for you. I expect she's looking for you right now."

"No she's not." he stated matter-of- factly, but he went out of the door anyway.

I really don't care where he went.

"Okay, Mrs. Trimble. Where were we? Danielle when your mother calls at six will you get up, get your shower, get dressed and catch the bus?"

"I'll try," Danielle replied.

"Not good enough, Danielle. Will you promise your mother you will get up, get dressed, and catch the bus?"

"Okay, yes," Danielle agreed.

"Good. I have a contract here that all three of us will sign. It states that you agree to this plan. If you are sick, you will bring a doctor's excuse to my office. Anytime you miss, I will call your mother at work."

"You know I can't take calls at work, Danielle," her mother reminds her.

"What do you think, Mrs. Trimble?"

"I'll try anything… that might work. Can't do nothing without your schooling. I wish I had got past high school. But at the rate she's going, she won't ever get her diploma," she shook her head.

"How about it?" I looked Danielle in the eye. "If you sign this contract your mother and I are going to hold you to it."

"I'll do it. I want to have a 'C' average so I can go out for the softball team this spring."

"Good. Right now, you don't have that 'C' average. Tell your teachers you know you have fallen behind, but you want to catch up. Ask them what you might do to bring those grades up. I'll tell Coach Young to talk to you about what position you would like to play. And Danielle, dress out for P.E. Anything else on your mind, Mrs. Trimble?…"

Before she had time to answer, I continued, "Help me keep her feet to the fire." I turned around to make copies. "Here's the contract signed by all of us, a copy for each of you."

"Thank you," the mother said, "I've already had to see the judge because my boy was missing too much, up there at the high school in the ninth grade. Judge Neman. He's a good fella. Tries to keep up with these young'uns. What was your name?"

"Orchard. Just like the apple orchard."

I looked at the stacks of papers spread over my desk, over my nameplate, over everything. Mostly discipline referrals. How could I stockpile this boodle of "In Progress" in just a few days? If all these pages suddenly took on a life of their own and creeped over to my chair to grab me by the neck.... Cause of death: disorganization. I've been watching too many British mysteries.

"And Ma'am," Mrs. Trimble turned as she was going out of the door, "I'm glad I don't have your job."

"Yes, Ma'am. Thank you."

Suddenly I realized that Josie had not come back.

Good.

I took a deep breath. My hand was shaking as I picked up a bottle of water from the desk and tried to reflect. I looked at the mound on my desk. Agnes came in with two more discipline referrals. P*eople work is always going to be messy. It ain't pretty. You already knew that. Very little ends up in the 'is done' pile. No instant gratification with this age group. I should have gone to FBI school to prepare for this job. I spend all day trying to find out, 'who done it.'*

It must be nice to be a judge who can take her gavel, pound it on the podium high in the air, and dare the kid to show their face back in her courtroom—or they will be put on a CINS (Child In Need of Supervision) petition and wash dishes at the Strickland Youth Center all weekend.

This program gave a parent a voluntary stopgap if their child was having problems at home and problems at school—before they got into the court system. They were sent to the Youth Center on weekends, assigned a counselor and shown what the next step would be if they kept acting out in oppositional ways. 'Youth Center' sounds innocuous, but in reality, it was a total lock down, a kid's jail, for those who would harm themselves or others.

Ten breaths in…ten breaths out. This job is not so bad. I worried that I would not see the kids enough. I see them all right, the same ones over and over again.

I ate breakfast at five a.m. and my stomach was growling. When I pulled out the bottom file drawer to find a snack, eek!!! Mice were gnawing around the edges of the sandwich I brought for lunch. They scurried away. Good. Fewer Weight Watcher points. What else could happen today for god's sake?

My speakerphone lit up: Mr. Black. "Mrs. Orchard."

"Yes?"

"It's 10:45, time for lunch duty in the cafeteria."

"Already? Yes, sir."

Sixth graders, first lunch wave. The teachers got a rest and ate lunch in the lounge. *Why do schools still have these long awkward picnic tables with seats connected on each side just like in the 50s and 60s?* After seventh grade, I could never figure out how to contort my body into a little ball and swing around to tuck my long legs under the table.

I became discombobulated—no, humiliated—if I had to ask a whole row of eighth grade boys to scoot down to let me in.

There must have been sixty of those tables full of kids in the noisy cafeteria at Parker. The serving line and drinks up front. No salad bar. Part of my post was to see that no one broke up in the queue. *I know, Americans say ' line,' but I feel so European when I say 'queue.'* If my job was in London, where we vacationed this summer, I would not have this chore. It is unthinkable to slip around someone in a queue in Europe in hopes that nobody notices. You would have ten people yell at you, then pick you up and put you at the end of the line or call the palace guards.

Unfortunately, our cowboy culture has continued, 'every man for himself.' If a sixth grade boy was bigger than the boy ahead of him, he would simply move in front of him and give him the stink eye. If that didn't work, a variation, not quite as harmonious, was to slap the little shrimp in front of you on the head, then move around him. It didn't matter to a sixth grader, unless I caught him and made him wash all the tables before he could eat.

I'm going to stand here for two and a half hours every day to be sure no one breaks up in the line? Living across the pond began to look like a viable option.

Jarred from my reverie, "Hi, Mrs. Orchard."

It was Mrs. Field.

She asked, "Did you bring your lunch today? Most of us do because we get too fat on this great home cookin.' The big, white rolls are sticky and gooey, each brown top lapped with butter."

"Hi, Mrs. Field. My lunch? I'm not sure you want to know. How is the science department?"

"We're just trying to hold it together until we restructure into teams next year. We hope to get a lot more teaching done. Too many discipline problems." she complained.

"Those interrelationships will be the key to change—the bonding among team teachers and among your students." I said thoughtfully. "Hey, changing the subject, Mrs. Field, how does Portland, Oregon, sound to you in November, Mt. Hood, a Bloody Mary at the ski lodge? Huh? Huh?"

"How so?" she asked.

I was excited to tell her, "NMSA meets there this year! It will be all about team restructuring to meet students' belonging needs. And teachers' belonging needs too, for that matter. Middle school teachers get burned out very…Wait just a minute," I interrupted our conversation about the trip and moved toward the little girl with knotty blond hair. "I was standing here watching you. You have gone to get napkins five times. Now stay seated and eat." She looked up at me with sad eyes.

I turned back to the teacher, "Mr. Black is giving me the time off to go to this conference, and I asked if someone could go with me. You are on the restructuring team with the administrators to develop the changes, Mrs. Field. I'd like for you to go."

"Sure. I'd love to. How much money?"

"I will send a memo to you with the dates. Mr. Black said that the school would pay our registration for the conference, $225.00 each. I'm writing a grant to try to get some money for our airline tickets. And guess what? My sister lives in Portland. We can stay with her."

"Wow. I'm in." Mrs. Field perked up.

I looked at the professional teacher who gets to know each of her students, studies their needs. If she can get away with me and get revitalized, her enthusiasm will spread to the entire faculty and...

"Come here, son, I know you didn't throw that empty milk carton across the table at those girls. Am I invisible? I am standing right at the end of your table. Guess I'm invisible. See me when you put up your tray."

She's a smoker, that lovely Mrs. Field. I watched her as she left the cafeteria. *I worry about that low grinding cough and her raspy voice...*

Weekends were for sleeping. My friend Cathy started complaining that I don't answer my phone. "Come for a visit," I replied. "The telephone has a negative connotation for me these days. I'm on the phone or someone in the building is buzzing me every minute. Do you think parents call the assistant principal because they are happy about what's going on at the school?"

I could not predict nor could I presume to understand how constricted, how limited my career landscape would become when I walked into the door of Parker Middle. Clearly, management meant politics and I began to get pressure to see the world through a narrow lens.

If my working relationship with Mr. Black became untenable, he could do more than annoy me. He could deliver a permanent blow that would end my career. It became paramount that I get a positive recommendation from Principal Billy Black for the next three years, until I got tenure at this level. If I got demoted back to the classroom for any reason, I would be washed-up. I would have no appeal. My world had become very small, indeed.

Fear belied my simplest decision. My stomach was hesitant to trust Mr. Black. I kept pushing that secret back down. I had some clues early on that our values may come to blows.

That afternoon I sat in my office, all the students gone. I smiled to myself about a kid I met in the hall whose name was Natorious. I kept asking him how he spelled that. His best buddy, Jake, put his arm around him and said, "And he is too, Miss O!" and we laughed with Nat.

Josie's nickname for me stuck and I came to like it. I told Agnes, "Miss O, the Assistant Principal, would be a good title for a B-rated porno movie." *Anything that keeps me from taking myself too seriously.*

Every educator I know gets the Sunday night blues. Our gut reminds us that tomorrow we will give 100 percent of our physical and emotional energy away—to kids. We take our jobs personally. Now you know. That is why we are highly defensive if we are criticized. We figure we better *pretend* to be perfect for the public, the school board, the newspapers, the parents...

On Sunday nights after my promotion, my stomach started to ache with anxiety, more distress than the Sunday blues. Okay, God, I should have been careful what I asked for. My decision to leave teaching—something I loved— may have been the result of my big ego. The kids were still fun but adults and politics? I did not understand.

On Monday morning, a policeman scared me on the interstate while I was driving to work; pulled up right beside me and looked me in the eye—to decide if I was drunk. When I realized I was going about forty, I waved, "Hello. It's me. I'm just sleepy. Have a nice day." He drove off, thank goodness. Usually it was a speeding ticket. I could never get three years without a "conviction" so that my insurance went down.

A student once told me his uncle, who is a drug dealer, made $100,000 a year, "more than you make."

Ah. *I have to think of a good answer*. "Maybe, but I don't have to spend four or five years in jail each decade and I don't have to look in my rear view mirror to see if a policeman is following me to work." *Or do I?* I didn't mention my speeding tickets, chuckling to myself.

I am a morning person and my husband is a night owl, the secret to a successful marriage. But 4:30 a.m.—when I hit the shower and went out the door with a breakfast bar for my forty minute commute—was even early for me

Then I wrestled with my heavy wad of keys at the front door, in the dark, until I found the right one. I stayed tired. There were a number of students dropped off at six a.m. because their parents worked an early shift at the shipyard.

However, I liked the raise I got, about $20,000 more a year, when I got the job in administration. I traded up. My dark red Honda sedan had over 150 thousand miles. I took it in to Joe Bullard and said, "Put me in a nice ride." Joe knows how to do it. I drove out that day with a white, sporty two-door Acura, white leather seats, heated—that I bragged about—but hardly needed in this semitropical climate. Have you ever noticed that the boss on a construction job always has a white Chevrolet or GMC truck, four doors, leather interior? I was not quite the boss, but close to it. Now I had to keep this job.

When Agnes got in at the front desk, I stuck my head out of my office door and shouted, "Good morning. Hey, come out front and see my new car."

"Baby have you gone and bought a new car? You just won't do. What was wrong with that Honda? I wish you'da sold it to me."

I came in from showing off the new car and looked around "Mr. Black is late coming in this morning."

"Oh, he's going to be gone all week." Agnes said.

"All week? He didn't mention that to me Friday... that he would be gone all week. Where is he?" I leaned across the counter and looked her in the eye.

"He said he was going to some conference with the superintendent in Orlando. That's all I know, honey."

"Do you have a number where I can reach him? I mean in case of an emergency?"

She just looked at me, "You and Mr. Bruse will have it by yourselves this week."

I left and went into my office to triage my "In Progress" to see if anything struck me as urgent. Agnes said that Mr. Black would check in with us. *Check in with us? I've only been here a couple of months. I adore Mr. Bruse. He is the kindest man in the world, but he can sometimes miss important things. For god's sake, so can I!*

"Do you have Mr. Black's number in case of an emergency?" I buzzed Agnes and asked again.

She sounded apologetic, "I can try, but I can't always get him."

"You must be kidding, Agnes. It takes three of us to run this school."

"Just do the best you can, baby. You'll do fine. I'll help you. We'll all help you."

I sat back in my chair. *I need to rest. I want to call Bill, to say, "You won't believe this!" I don't even have the energy to 'awfulize.' It is awful. I need to focus on all this work.* I waved my hand over the desk.

The older women at church still referred to me as 'baby' or 'honey' or addressed my friends and me as 'you young girls.' I wanted to say to Agnes, "Gee, I'm forty-five. When do I qualify to be an adult?"

I have made it until Friday. Nothing too bad happened this week.

The faucet was left on in the boys' bathroom on 'B' hall and water came out on the carpet a couple of feet. The fan should dry it out by Monday.

It was 10:45, already time for cafeteria duty. I bought lunch every day after I found out I'd have to share my bag lunch with the mice. I began eating the big buttery rolls. Anxiety.

When I got to the cafeteria the women behind the steam table were mopping up water; a small pipe burst. What is it with water this week? I stepped to the back and saw that the manager had it under control.

A tiny girl ran up behind me, and yanked on my navy skirt. "Somebody threw applesauce on me." When I looked up, a carrot flew by my head. *Oh shit.* I heard a loud rumbling—that meant trouble.

Carl and Gabe, two eighth grade boys, were standing up on the back table waving and yelling to the other kids to, "Go outside! Go outside!"

"Sit down Carl! Gabriel, go to my office!" I screamed. By this time they took off to the other end of the cafeteria by the door, grabbing milk cartons out of the cooler as they ran outside. "Sit down everybody!" Many of the girls complied. If students heard a loud call from a familiar voice or if they heard a crashing thump when a book was slammed on the floor, that was often enough to make them pause. It was too late.

"You're short life is going to be over if you don't sit down!" I yelled.

"SHUT UP!" I heard a loud voice right behind me.

"What!" I turned around. It was Billy Black. He appeared out of nowhere at noon on Friday. *Thanks a lot! I'm sure he did not tell me to SHUT UP! a professional educator in his building.* My whole body burned red. Fire was in my gut when I looked at him. My muscles tensed in attack mode. I clenched my fists.

I did not confront him. But the hate that rose up in me that day had no place to go and never went away.

"Give me the walkie-talkie, Mrs. Orchard." Mr. Black said. "Coaches. All coaches report to the cafeteria, please."

He spoke in such a pleasant voice you might think he was inviting the coaches to a nice lunch in the cafeteria. Billy Black's highest value: always keep your cool. Never show your real feelings to students and teachers.

I ran outside to see what I could do. The seventh grade boys formed in a long line in the schoolyard facing the eighth grade boys standing in a long line against the building. Just as I came out of the door—whop—I got hit in the neck with a full milk carton, milk sloshing all over me. It was cannon battery fire.

Coach Lane came out and caught my arm. "You better go in Mrs. Orchard. You're going to get hurt. We'll get 'em in."

Oh, shit. I'm shaken…scared. I am about to get hurt. I am hurt.

What just happened? Things got out of control so quickly. I was chilled, ready to collapse, from the emotional and physical trauma when I finally got into my office. I tried to dry some of the milk off of my skirt and grabbed my blue blazer off the coat rack to hide most of the wet spots.

I didn't know I would be in physical danger when I got this job. What was I thinking?

I ran to the mirror behind the door to see if my neck was bleeding. It was throbbing. No blood. Good. But there was a red abrasion on the left side of my neck, a large vein raised, blue/black. It was a direct hit. I was not the target. I had just stepped out of the door. *I'll put some makeup over the bright red spot tomorrow. I don't want students laughing about hitting an adult.*

Yes, I saw red, but it was mostly anger, rage. I could not even cry. Not yet.

Before I knew it, I picked up a small pillow from my chair and began hurling it, a fast pitch against the wall over and over and over again until I was out of breath. Exhausted, I fell to the floor. The tears flowed uncontrollably and I moaned with pain, a groan that I had not heard since my father's tragedy ten years before.

I looked around. *What am I doing on the floor? I've got to get up before Agnes comes in. She'll think I've cracked-up. I have cracked up!* I managed a slight smile as I struggled to get off the floor. *It's more difficult than it was when I was teaching. I don't function well when I feel physically and emotionally unsafe.*

This was my job. I didn't want the coaches to take care of the emergency*—and certainly not Mr. Black. Where did he come from? Suddenly he was right behind me—granted not one of my best moments. But what nerve! Mr. Super Cool came in to save the day*. I wanted to hurt him, bad.

I'm going down to the central office and report that he told me to "Shut up." That will be in his file.

I forgot one detail. The superintendent was one of Billy Black's best friends. They coached a successful football team together at Mulberry High.

I dangled out on a precarious limb. It would not be the last time.

Dr. Cromwell came through the door with the x-rays, slapped them on the light board, pulled the stool over and propped his long legs up on the counter, satisfied.

"Stand up, turn around and face the wall, Mrs. Orchard. Let me see you put your arms up as high as you can."

"My gown comes open in the back."

He jumped down. "I'll hold your gown. Just raise your arms up high. Oh. I see. Not very far. Hmm. This type of thing can happen after an accident or an injury. Are you sure there's been no injury to your shoulders, maybe a whiplash or a fall?"

"I don't know. No. I don't think so."

"Or someone with a disease, family history of avascular…?"

I drifted off to that gray noise in my head…ZZZZZZ…

Suddenly I blocked out the doctor's words with the words of my Daddy coming in from work when I was a little girl, *"Why are your shoulders so red, Donna?"*

Dr. Cromwell turned around on the stool to look at me, "Are you following me, Mrs. Orchard?"

"Oh. 'a' what?"

"It's one word— *avascular,"* he said.

"Then it's something about my blood?"

"Avascular necrosis is a fancy way of saying that the cells in your shoulders are dying, have frozen up, but I have no idea why."

"I know why." I countered.

"Well, good. I'm trying to get at that. "

"I raise my shoulders up and stiffen my neck when my boss buzzes my office. I notice that. Ah. He hates me. I act nice. I act business-like. I act feminine. I stay away from him. He still hates me."

"Okay. I got it. Stress. I don't think you can narrow your own blood vessels, Mrs. Orchard. The blood supply is actually diminished here in this bone tissue, he pointed to the x-ray; why you can't raise your arms. Now what we need to do is…"

I drifted off again… ZZZZZZ…

"Did you leave these children in the park again all day, Marion? Look at Donna's shoulders." Daddy was angry.

"Mrs.Orchard, did you hear what I said about the surgery, about decompression?"

"About surgery? Say that again."

"Well, I haven't actually tried this on shoulders, but it works effectively on hips. I'll put you to sleep, take a long needle and put little holes into the bones of both your shoulders. It will trick the body into reacting as though there is a fracture. The blood supply will then move into these tiny holes in order to heal the tissue."

I've always been a sucker for tall and smart. He looked handsome with his legs stretched up on that counter.

He continued, "I'm a teaching doc out at South, at the University. You'll be my first shoulders."

"Something very bad must have happened in your childhood to cause you to get so excited about cutting on people and sticking them with needles. Just kidding, Doc. I trust you. You've fixed me up a couple of times."

Parker Middle 1993

I was determined that second year to improve my working relationship with Billy Black. The restructuring plan he organized the previous year was a good one and promised to create a better, healthier school. We had some common ground.

I was surprised and pleased when Mr. Black asked me to prepare a presentation to the faculty with regard to the new program. I thought about it for days and made notes to try to cover some of the more subtle advantages of the changes.

We had a great faculty who should be thanked for the new program and the many hours of organization that it took to open school smoothly with an improved infrastructure.

Let me think. I need an icebreaker. The teachers will be hungry after school. perfect. I'll dig out my recipe and serve Mexican layered dip—even print some copies if anyone wants one.

Sylvia's Refried Bean Platter

1. One can refried beans (sprinkle with garlic salt and cumin)
2. Two avocados made into guacamole
3. One c. sour cream
4. 3/4 c. salsa
5. One c. sharp grated cheddar cheese
6. 1/3 c. finely chopped onion
7. One c. shredded lettuce
8. 1/3 c. chopped green pepper
9. 1/3 c. chives or chopped green onion bottoms
10. One small can ripe olives
11. One tomato chopped (sprinkle with salt and pepper)
12. Optional: ½ c. minced cilantro

Spread beans on platter; leave 1 ½ inches from the edge.

Spread mashed avocado (with lemon juice, a little mayonnaise) on top of beans.
Spread sour cream on top of avocado.
Spread on salsa, then onion.
Sprinkle on ½ of cheese.
Sprinkle on lettuce with #8, 9, 10, 11, and 12.
Sprinkle on remainder of cheese and cilantro on top of all.
Serve with hardy crackers.

At the faculty meeting Monday afternoon, I said, “Go ahead and enjoy your snacks while I begin.” The teachers looked rested from the summer, the women in neat collared blouses and flats, the men in new khaki Dockers and colorful button downs. We were all in a good mood and Billy Black hung around and listened to what I had to say.

I began my presentation. “Mr. Black shared this restructuring plan with me when I came to Parker last year as assistant principal. We would like to thank him for this forward-thinking idea and the willingness to spend hours in the planning and implementation. *Applause*. And give yourselves a hand. *More applause.* As far as I know, we are the first school to implement the Model Middle School program in this county and…”

The talk went well. I may have even picked up some brownie points from Mr. Black.

I continued to avoid him when possible and it was several days before I saw Mr. Black coming down the hall toward me. He was a short, chunky man who seemed puffed up with his own importance, his tie sticking straight out in the middle. *Men immediately size up their suitability for each woman they meet. I suspect Billy Black recoils from me unconsciously. It works both ways.*

I smiled in anticipation when I saw Mr. Black, certain that I would get some good feedback on my presentation to the faculty.

I had not admitted, even to myself, that I was loaded and cocked. For a year I had trapped my fear and anger in my shoulders, crammed his scorn, his scowl, his lack of respect way down in my gut. " *I hired Mrs. Orchard because she had the best legs",* he told my teacher friends. Then after I had run the school for a week, he came in and yelled at me to *"Shut Up!"* This disgraced me in front of the kids. He called Josie, *"crazy,"* Mr. Buse, *"worthless."* In the teacher's lounge, he presented me with a mess of crawfish for a 'Christmas present' and asked me, *"Do you suck heads, Mrs. Orchard*?" All the teachers laughed—he is the principal—at his sick brand of humor.

I have the remainder of this year and next year before I get tenured. I cannot confront him…cannot…cannot…cannot…

Repressing his obvious contempt. I was a cornered animal.

I came face to face with Mr. Black in the hall, "Hi Mr. Black. Uh. What did you think of my presentation?"

He frowned and gave me the familiar disgusted look, "Mrs. Orchard, don't use *I, I, I,* all the time. You need to use *'we.'*

The smoldering fear that I pushed down in my gut for over a year suddenly came up in my throat and began to choke me. My rule for myself was NPO (nil per oram), nothing by mouth. I would never write anything or say anything to Black to give him reason to fire me.

Suddenly I was in Billy Black's face, an observer, as I heard my own voice unrestrained, defiant, yelling. "That's it! I can't do anything to please you! I worked on the presentation for three days!"

I noticed that Josie—in the hall of course—stopped to stare at us when I raised my voice, then other teachers and students stopped to see what the yelling was about.

He dropped to a whisper, "Mrs. Orchard, you can't stop in the hall and yell at me in front of the students and faculty. I'll take care of this."

You do that Mr. Cool!

I lurched forward in a flight of panic. When I flung myself into the car I started looking around for a box cutter, some scissors, anything. I was a helpless little girl again turning my hatred in on myself, trapped inside my own head. Depression was common to me but I had never experienced fantasies of suicide. *Oh, God. I need some help.* I was caught in a deadfall confronted with two irreconcilable demands.

I don't remember driving to Bayview Mental Health Center, but I do remember bolting in screaming, "I'm going to hurt myself! Please help me." Everyone in the waiting room, some with puffy red eyes, fell silent and stared at me.

The door opened from the back and I slumped toward the nurse. She was in a blue lab coat, her badge: *Psychiat-*

ric Nurse Practitioner. Her eye was sharp, her facial expression neutral.

" He... Job... Fired... I want to die. Help me! I want to die. I'm going to hurt myself if you don't help me."

"Umm. Sit down and wait a minute. Try to calm down. Sit right here by me. What's your name?"

"Donna Orchard. You don't understand I want to kill myself!"

"Did something happen? Did you have an event?" she asked.

Crying. Crying. Crying. Sobbing. Low, gut wrenching sobs. "I...I...I... yelled at my boss. I'm scared. I've never wanted to kill myself. Can you help me? I'm really, really scared. I'm going to be fired. I've been to school all my life—now I'm going to be fired. Do you understand I will have no appeal? I can't just go out and find another job!"

"Do you have a psychiatrist?" she asked.

"No."

"How about a family doctor?"

"Yes, Dr. Thomas."

"Where is he located?"

"Daphne. David, David Thomas. Can I lie down? I want to pull something over my head."

"Just a minute. Let me see if I can get Dr. Thomas' nurse. *Hello? I have a patient of Dr. Thomas' here at Bayview in Mobile. Donna Orchard...Yes. Distraught. Yes. Work related. Any diagnosis, history of this type of thing? No obvious disability? What about diabetes? No. Antidepressants? Yes. Okay. Thank you.*"

She turned to me, "Have you been taking your anti-depressants?"

"Oh, yes. I never miss."

"Okay, Donna, you seem to be a little calmer now. You can make an appointment with one of our counselors today or choose someone else. I'd advise you to seek some help, to find someone to talk to. You can go as soon as you feel calm enough to drive."

"What?"

I was back at work the next morning opening the door at six o'clock. I didn't know what else to do. *I'm not going to be fired for failure to do my job.* I avoided Mr. Black the whole day waiting for my call from the Central Office. About three, I got the call to come down immediately and talk to Mr. Leonard, Assistant Superintendent.

The decision for both of us: "You'll stay together this year and work out your problems."

That's it? I'm not fired?

Chapter 12
BUILDING TOLERANCE

Parker Middle School
1994

Kathy James was one of those friends, teachers often are, who could bring a drill over to help me hang curtains or bring her sound advice over to help me write a grant. My second year at Parker I submitted what I hoped was a strong proposal to International Paper Company, to implement a program entitled Building Tolerance.

My third year began with a boon. I got a letter saying we got the grant— over $9,000 from the International Paper Company Foundation—for a conflict resolution program! Even Billy Black understood money, $9,000 for his school. *Maybe I'm no longer in the doghouse.*

The notion of a practical program to deal with conflict was not a vagary. It had not come to me subtly, but starkly, when I was called to the breezeway during recess the previous year.

A middle schooler who gets on the bus with a knife or a gun will usually show it to at least one person. Hopefully the driver gets wind of it and administrators are waiting at the bus to check book bags. The student who is afraid, who is bullied, is the one who typically brings a weapon to protect themselves, to scare someone away.

We missed this one. A fight had been brewing over a boy. One eighth grade girl stabbed another in the gut with a three-inch blade at Parker. When I came out of the door on the north breezeway, she dropped the knife and a quick-witted teacher put her foot on the weapon. The injury was serious, but not life threatening. I had no trouble identifying the unusual knife in court, a thick ornate inlayed handle, silver snakes going around and around. I had never broached this kind of violence in my twenty years as an educator in urban schools. The Mobile Police Department took care of the case and I expelled the perpetrator from public schools.

"Conflict resolution. That is where we must begin," I told Kathy when we initially discussed the grant proposal. The violence the year before had shocked me, a stark reminder that everyday disagreements, allowed to fester, routinely resulted in suspensions, valuable days spent out of school and could even lead to serious injury or death.

I sold my lunch tray to him for $1.00 and he never paid me…

I lost my book and she has it. I know what my book looks like…

She's spreading rumors about me, that I had sex with that boy…

I sat down with him on the bus and he moved. He told everybody I stink. I have to sit by myself and...

He keeps sticking me in the back with a pencil until I let him ahead of me in line...

Her group of girls keep calling me names and saying they are going to beat me up if I don't stay away from Jimmy...

He said my mother is so fat she can't get out of the car to come into the school...

Parker was overcrowded. Built for 800, we had 1300 students enrolled. The main purpose of the Building Tolerance program must be to communicate to the school community that making Parker safe was everyone's responsibility.

Eighth graders were trained to be peer mediators, student leaders who would be positive influences in the school. These students, some of them at risk themselves, were trained to help their peers talk out their problems: 1) define the problem 2) brainstorm possible solutions and 3) evaluate solutions, choose one, and act on it.

T-shirts were the first step when working with middle schoolers—right after food. The light blue shirts with dark blue letters *Building Tolerance* were encircled on the front with the three steps in peer mediation.

The justice department sent a team from Atlanta to train the student mediators at an intensive two-day workshop at the Holiday Inn with *lunch provided*. The school found a room near the office to conduct mediations.

Victor was a popular football player, raised by his grandparents, who engaged me in conversation in the hall daily. I related to him because I was brought up by my grandparents and preferred talking with adults when I was a kid. Victor was totally trustworthy. "Will you be the captain of the student mediator team?" I asked him."

"Yes!"

He worked behind the scenes assigning a mediator to take two students who were arguing to mediation. If there was a successful outcome, there was no reason for me to become involved.

As a result, the classrooms became more peaceable as the students became aware that they had conflicts. Then there was another option—to ask for help—before they were referred to the principal's office.

The mediators kept the 'conflict escalator' in front of them during a mediation to keep track of which way the response was moving.

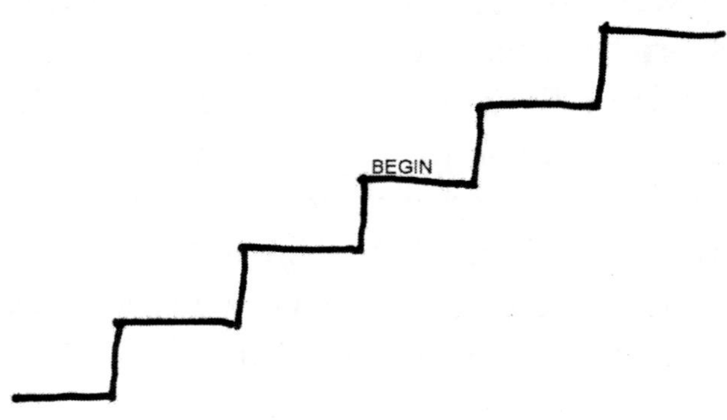

- Every behavior that makes the conflict worse will take it another step up the escalator.
- The higher you go on the escalator, the harder it is to come down.

Agnes buzzed my office: "Lieutenant Saul Briggs from the Mobile Police Department is here to see you, Mrs. Orchard."

"Thank you, Agnes. Send him in."

When I looked up from my desk, there was an expansive presence that filled the room. About 6' 3" tall, his shirt and tie framed husky shoulders. On one side of his belt was a gleaming gold badge, on the other side, the handle of a small revolver hidden in a black leather holster. I remembered Lt. Briggs from the year before when he investigated the stabbing incident. We met again in court at the trial. We liked each other. His warmth had depth.

Lt. Briggs would be just the right person to conduct the parenting sessions, another component of the grant. Familiar with the neighborhood and some of the parents, he was someone who could talk to the mothers, fathers, grandparents of our students about healthy problem solving with their teenagers.

The big guy with a big heart held two parenting workshops during the year to discuss concerns brought up by the parents: making curfew work the first time, parenting kids that employers will want to hire, staying calm when kids do incredibly upsetting things... He was a key contributor to positive community publicity throughout the year of the grant and maximized a positive attitude toward law enforcement agencies and those in authority.

I had to look at the polished badge when he was around. *Why do women love uniforms?*

I got the idea that Principal Billy Black thought that I should hand him the check for $9,000 to use at his discretion. He ignored the program all together except for one comment, "You have not made me aware of anything you have planned."

My plans were on his desk for every activity, on or off campus and the dates. He did not buy into the program and there were never any referrals for peer mediation from his office.

This was my third year as an assistant principal. I had to begin a fourth year before I got tenure. Near the end of that year, I found out a week before the board meeting that Billy Black recommended to the board that I not receive tenure, which meant being sent back into the classroom.

I went to the superintendent with stacks of notebooks and evidence that I had done my job at Parker for three years. He had already made his decision based on Mr. Black's recommendation and refused to look at any of my materials. He sat behind his big desk and looked at me.

I went to the teacher's union representative and he told me I had no appeal if I was not tenured. He could not help me.

Then I remembered the big man, the handsome police lieutenant who wore the impressive badge at his side. We instantly related to each other and had lots of fun planning the parenting component of the Building Tolerance program. He was sincere and kind, but knew when to be firm with the parents. I thought that he could be an advocate, ally, if he was willing to speak in my support at the meeting. He was shocked that Mr. Black was trying to fire me and at the last hour, the last minute, before I got tenure.

"Of course, I'll be there." He communicated with the minority members of the board and let them know that he was prepared to speak.

Bill and I sat in the back of the crowded boardroom. I didn't see Lt. Briggs. *I'm sure I told him the time.* The nameplates for the board members were there, an equal minority/majority board and the superintendent who gave his recommendation, but who did not vote. The chairs were still empty a few minutes after the start time. *My stomach* has b*een aching for days. I'm glad it will be over tonight—whatever the outcome.*

Bill—my husband in a second marriage—reached for my hand. "You're pale, honey. You shouldn't even be here! I'm pissed. All the hours you've put in at that school…"

"Hush." I whispered. "The board is being seated."

There was other business about the renovation of Barton Academy, the historical Central Office, those speaking for and against. *It's going on forever.* I looked around but the Lieutenant was not there. *He's not coming.*

A few principalships were announced then: Donna Orchard, Assistant Principal at Parker Middle School recommendation for nontenure.

"Suddenly I heard Lt. Briggs' strong voice from the back, "Madame President, I wish to address the board." All eyes were on him.

"The board recognizes Lt. Saul Briggs, an investigator with the Mobile County Police Department." The president nodded when he got to the podium. "Mr. Briggs."

"Madam President, board members, and superintendent: I have known Mrs. Orchard for two years. I met her first when I investigated an incident at Parker Middle School in 1992. She contacted me at the beginning of this year to participate with her in the parenting component of a grant that she wrote for the school. I suggested that we invite groups of parents to discussions of topics such as respect, patience, honesty, humility, compassion and aggression as they affected their relationship with their teenagers. We had question and answer sessions on patterns that parents had established with their children. Personally I have found Mrs. Orchard to be thoughtful, intelligent, and fair with peers and students.

This year alone, the Building Tolerance grant brought in over $9,000 for Parker Middle, to give the school extra services that the state could not provide. The peer mediation program has been a success in teaching students how to solve problems without violent words or actions. The numbers of officers called to this school is down this year which I attribute to some of Mrs. Orchard's initiatives…"

It was beautiful. As the crowd watched Lt. Briggs walk from the front, there was an aura of positive energy that dominated the room. He prevailed. We prevailed. I kept my job.

Assistant Principal with Davenport Band

Chapter 13
SILVER MAPLES

1996

Davenport Magnet School for the Performing Arts

Margie Eva Castleberry prattled to plants. When she thinned her flower garden in the spring, she appeared in my yard unannounced, fingernails black with dirt, to pass along red spider lilies, yellow/orange gladiola bulbs and white Easter lilies. Flowers bloomed upon her command. Yellow, red, and purple blossoms picked up their heads, smiled in her direction as she came down the walk, knowing she would put her nose ever so close to examine each particular microcosm.

After four years at Parker middle school, working for Billy Black, I heard of a vacancy: Assistant Principal at Davenport Magnet School for the Performing Arts. I knew the principal and even though he was very slow in making a decision, I got the job after school started in 1996.

This was one of the best middle schools in the county and one in which I could acquire professional distinction. Finally, all of my hard work at Parker had paid off with a new assignment that was a move up.

I was a singer and played clarinet in high school and more recently became interested in the visual arts, developing friendships with several local artists. *An arts school. Yes! This is where I was meant to be.*

Davenport School was a lovely, safe school with a staff of some of the finest preforming arts teachers in Mobile. There were 450 students compared to the Parker's 1300. *I will not have to spend all day with discipline referrals. I can be a curriculum specialist instead of an investigator. Nothing too bad could happen here.*

Each student was required to take two performing arts classes. Hence, the school was alive with the sights and sounds of children dancing, singing, and playing horns; tiny ballerinas on tippy toes ran down the hall in pink tights and tutus topped with sparkling feathery headbands; a black and white photography exhibit covered the wall—what every school should be. An unusual configuration, grades four through eight, there was a kind of single-minded energy at every level. The end- of- the- year programs were legendary: ballet, jazz band, choir and visual arts. A crowd from the whole area filled the gym.

Arts teachers had singular beliefs, convictions, and expectations. The principal reined them in at times to reestablish a balance with the academic curriculum.

The assistant principal was often a liaison between the teachers and the principal. Teachers tended to gripe and fuss to the assistant principal about school problems in an 'us against them' scenario. The teachers saw that I was more like them, more accessible to them. It was a game. We all played. They could not go to the principal with all of their complaints, but they could come to me.

There was a small dusty spot at the school where the students stood each day to catch their rides home. I watched them for a year bake in the sultry sun of the Gulf Coast. *The space might be big enough for a couple of trees. But what kind?* I wanted a tree that grew fast. This was not a budgeted item so I dug down in my own pocket.

"Silver maples grow fast, Margie Eva said, "the undersides of the leaves are like stars fluttering in the breeze, a perfect tree to shade the children."

My favorite garden phrase is "I have more time than I have money." Affordable at the garden shop were two small silver maples, which I planted, closely following Margie's recipe:

1. Dig the hole twice as large as the pot the tree is growing in.
2. Mix some Black Cow fertilizer with the dirt.
3. Fill the hole with water.
4. Loosen the roots when it comes out of the pot.
5. Put the tree in the muddy hole and cover with the soil mixture up to where it was growing in the pot. Caution: no deeper.
6. Mulch around the trunk with pine straw.

Two students, Ann and Kaleb agreed to come get the watering can from my office and keep the trees moist for at least first two weeks. "Chances are, I'll forget."

School desegregation remained a complex endeavor in Mobile. There was little support for requiring mandatory student reassignments, such as busing students for the sole purpose of racial balance. The residential neighborhoods were largely segregated. The white parents wanted their children to have the curriculum in this performing arts school. The black parents wanted their underperforming downtown schools in their neighborhoods improved. In particular, the development of magnet schools allowed for voluntary desegregation after decades of forced integration failed to eliminate one-race schools.

John LeFlore, an activist in the Civil Rights Movement in Mobile, filed suit to desegregate Mobile Public Schools (Birdie Mae Davis v. the Board of Education) in 1963. The case remained active until its dismissal in 1997, the longest running secondary desegregation suit in U.S. history. This was one year after I came to Davenport Magnet as an assistant principal.

What made magnet schools successful other than the curriculum? Each child had at least one responsible adult; a mom, grandmother, uncle, who wanted them in the school and took the time to fill out the application. The students were then chosen through an impartial lottery system, the names picked at random. The school adhered to a strict 50-50 ratio of minority/majority population. A student must have at least a 'C' average and agree to enroll in two performing arts classes each year, requirements to remain in the school.

Fifteen years after I retired, I went back to visit Davenport. As I headed for the double doors I had unlocked on so many mornings, my eyes went straight up—the two silver maples! The trees blessed by Margie Eva Castleberry were now vaulting into the blue sky over the ten-foot chain link fence. The graceful leaves shimmered silver as they twirled and twisted in the wind like the petite ballerina's pirouette.

I gazed up through the branches and thought of my own reflection, my hair now dusted with silver threads. The memories came back, overwhelming me like a turbulent flood— the crushing blow that came two years after the trees were planted. I sat on the curb and cried.

Chapter 14
STRAWHEADS

1999

I locked the door behind me while working alone in the summertime. It was after five o'clock before I called security to tell them I was leaving the building. I pushed the inside lock on the door and stood outside to twirl the hefty set of keys. Finding the small silver one for the padlock hanging on a chain—snap. *Shake it. Be sure it's locked.*

It was one of those serendipitous moments.

I turned around and there, standing on the downtown street corner were my boss, Dr. Barker, the superintendent of the County Public School System and Mr. Monroe, a principal I knew. Both in dark suits, they looked up when I banged out of the door at Davenport Magnet. *I'm glad Dr. Barker sees me coming out of the school at five o'clock in the afternoon in the summer. He knows I'm an assistant principal willing to get the job done, to get the school ready to open*—after the untimely resignation of the principal in July.

Mr. Mason, the popular principal, left to take a high school job in another county.

I glanced down at the corner again and saw the two men standing on the curb talking. Figuring I had nothing to lose, *I'll approach Dr. Barker to see if he will give me a thumbs up about the principalship at Davenport or at least give me some encouragement that I will be his recommendation tomorrow at the board meeting..*

I wanted it. I was excited with the possibility of getting this principalship in a magnet school, a flagship middle school. The principalship at the school was traditionally a black male position since the school opened as a Junior High many years before. The change into a performing arts magnet came in 1992 maintaining a 50-50 ratio of white and black; however, the tradition of a black male principal remained. My only hope was that the top job had come open suddenly and the board would consider a white female in a pinch.

The agenda for the school board meeting was in the Mobile Press-Register; therefore, I knew that the Davenport principalship would be announced the next day.

Even though I was getting the school ready to open, no one had called to discuss the principalship with me or ask if I would take it. I had no interview with the superintendent. Appointments were decided through hearsay—who said what about this person or that person, who liked whom, who was rumored a racist, or not... The name was withheld even from the person who was recommended until the appointments were announced in the newspaper the next morning.

I walked down the sidewalk toward the two men. "Hello, Dr. Barker, Mr. Monroe."

"Hello, Mrs. Orchard." I had never had a conversation with the superintendent so I knew Mr. Monroe must have told him who I was.

After chatting about the loss of a colleague and the funeral they were attending at the church down the street, and the weather...

"Dr. Barker, I really like this school. I am very happy. I would like to be the principal." I said.

"I have a recommendation on the agenda for the board tomorrow." He looked at me with surprise and disgust. My loyalty had come into question. I had ignored the sacrosanct network of secrets when I asked for information about a job. It would not be forgiven.

"Um m. Okay. Thank you very much. Nice to see you both."

His scorn scared me. What I asked Dr. Barker may have been awkward and ill timed, a little Pollyannaish—but nobody was dead! *It's no time for jokes.*

I sat down on a bench beside the silver maples. *I need to stop holding my breath. There is nothing I can do about it now.*

I looked high over my head to the top of the trees. They were growing, those small maples, happy in their new little dusty home, shimmering. That's what this school was all about: silver trumpets and long gold trombones; jazz dancers with white glittery eye shadow, silver top hats over red sequins for the holidays...I imagined all of the girls financing college at NYU by dancing with the Rockettes at Radio City Music Hall.

I smiled as I thought about how I was particularly thankful for trombones. This year, early one morning, I was working before school started when tiny Ella came running into my office out of breath.

"Johnathan let some boys string him up on the flag pole, Mrs. Orchard! Put the rope in the back of his shirt. They thought it would be funny. They didn't get far. Don't worry. He's alright. When he fell, he fell right into his open trombone case. He didn't get hurt."

All the parents were up at the school before the bell rang for first period.

I had been an assistant principal for seven years, four years at Parker and three at Davenport Magnet when this principalship came open. If I got the appointment, it would be an irregular appointment. Assistant principals were generally moved to a different school to begin the principalship where the new person and staff held no preconceived notions, to give the new principal a fresh start.

Having a conversation with my husband, undeniably an intellectual, "Donna, you are visual, an artist. You will never fit in with the linear world." His words were incoherent nonsense at the time. I was in a trajectory resistant to any idea that I had a choice about the job if it was offered me. If I turned down this principalship, after all the student loans through all these years—it would be crazy. The teachers and staff at Davenport knew me. What could go wrong?

When women got passed over for secondary administrative promotions, our aspirations and eagerness often gave way to a hopelessness: we were not winning football coaches, we did not have as much upper body strength as a man to break up fights, and we did not want the reputation of sleeping our way to the top.

One day while whining to myself, it came to me—the real reason men got the top jobs—canoogling. They canoogled on the golf course. They canoogled in neighborhood bars over a couple of beers, at meetings, at parties...

Women, we need to learn how to canoogle.

Because of growing up in an alcoholic home— *I'm not that important;* nevertheless, I was the only thing I ever thought about. Then in the next moment, I felt like I didn't deserve to take up space in the world or breathe anyone's air.

However, I pushed past these obvious impediments to canoogling and let some of my friends at the Central Office know of my desire for the Davenport job.

Clearly, I was getting the school ready to open in five weeks. It would be a vote of 'no confidence' if Dr. Barker gave the principalship to someone else—to train.

Family matters led women to come into school administration at a much older age than their male counterparts, even close to fifty-years-old, as was my case.

Men, with an intent to go into administration, often taught the required three years and became assistant principals. It was complex. *Some* coaches, in spite of the reputation, did have the qualifications to become effective principals: organizational skills, motivational skills, and contact with the public. Being a winning football coach was, and still is, the fast track to the top high school jobs for top pay in the South.

The next day in the Mobile Press-Register the principalship was announced: Donna Orchard, Principal, Davenport Magnet School for the Performing Arts.

"Yes!" I hugged Bill.

My friend, Carroll sent a lovely hanging fern to the school the next week, "Congratulations!"

I should be relaxed. I wasn't. There was that series of uneven events that brought me to this juncture. An assistant principal doesn't get a promotion to principal and stay in the same school *for a reason.* I knew that the appointment to Davenport came about because I could get the school open at the last minute—not because it was decided that this assignment was the best for the school or for me—principal by default. *I'll have to be irreproachable this first year to prove myself.*

Busy with scheduling , only one month after my appointment, there was a call from the Central Office to meet with the superintendent. *It couldn't be good.*

I had no idea why I was there when the secretary asked me to sit down in the outer office. I did take something to read, sure I would wait for a while, the appropriate amount of time one must wait to see an important person. Carl Sandburg wrote a poem entitled, "Waiting for the Big Man."

I called Joe, my buddy in Al-Anon, "I'm scared, all the secrecy."

Joe said, "Take all of us with you into that room. Imagine that we are sitting around you. Your angels."

That's a good thought. There are plenty of people who love me. I won't be alone. Sure. How much damage could I do in one month, anyway?

I need to be at school. I was in a time crunch to get the scheduling done. Grades 4-8 must have two performing arts classes scheduled around their core subjects, often a conundrum.

I shivered when I recalled the school board meeting when I was on the agenda to be fired by Billy Black right before I got tenure as assistant principal. *Is this the human condition; your mind goes back to the worst moment of your life right before the next ... worse moment of your life?*

I had to start tenure over again at the principal level. Three years. If anything happened and I lost my job, I would have to sell my house and move to another county or to another state to find another job, probably a teaching job at half the pay. It worked that way. If you did not make tenure at any level, especially administration, you were 'back balled" by every other school in the state and most of those out-of-state. The reality is: if you got fired as a principal, your career was over. Educators, in spite of their flexibility with children, can be harsh and unforgiving among themselves. Administrators were a small competitive community who carried the burden of trying to appear perfect to the public and to parents for fear of getting fired. This perfectionism flowed over to relationships with colleagues in a world that became increasingly isolated the higher you moved in management.

Why am I going there? I don't know what this meeting is about. I had one brief conversation with Dr. Barker on a downtown street corner about a month ago.

There was no orientation for new principals. I knew the basics: You don't want to get negative press about the school in the newspaper and you don't want to be called to the Central Office.

Before I had time to open my book, Dr. Barker rushed out of his door toward me red faced. "Get in here."

I looked around, "Pardon. Do you mean me?"

He was obviously angry. "Get in here, Mrs. Orchard."

Just a short time in Al-Anon, I learned that if a total stranger was raging at me, it had more to do with them than with me.

I quickly forgot this healthy thought when I was seated at the end of the large dark conference table, in the 'mush pot,' to the left of the superintendent's elbow.

It's like when I was about to have my first baby, when I thought it couldn't get any worse, my blood pressure dropped as the nurse stood talking about her weekend in New Orleans. She forgot about me until the machine started blaring.

That machine is blaring in my head right now. It was cold in the conference room as I shivered and looked around me. No angels, just Ph.D.s. Men in dark suits, women in dark suits circled the long mahogany table: Head of Human Resources, Head of the Magnet School Program. Head of Secondary Schools, Head of Student Services, many whom I had worked with at one time or another.

Why did they put me on this cold steel table with my feet up on sharp stirrups, leave me so exposed? Somebody put a blanket under me. Won't somebody help me?

Dr. James, don't you remember that we studied together for that final? Mrs. Kendrick, that program we designed is implemented and working well. Don't you remember?

I know why this is happening. I'm shy. Someone at a workshop told me that I didn't look people in the eye because I was shy. I never knew that. I should try to look these people in the eye.

I picked my head up and looked around the table again.

I get the opposite reaction from some people. I've been told I'm too assertive. Who am I? I can't figure it out.

All white collars and cuffs. They look like manikins. Dressed the same, no affect. I am not that important after only one month, to get all the suits together, suits that don't wrinkle at the elbow.

My sweaty hands were clammy on the chair. *Could I move, please? I am right under the air conditioner. That would not be allowed. Not here.*

I need to be back at school finishing the scheduling so I can get school open. I still don't have an assistant principal. I am usually successful at flying under the radar screen, until today. I work hard and people just leave me alone to do the work they don't want to do. All this attention gives me the creeps.

Excuse me nurse. I have changed my mind about having this baby. Would you hand me my clothes? My icy toes are frozen in these stirrups.

The manikins with strawheads were all the same, straw sticking out of the top of their heads in every direction, over pale lips and drawn faces. Emotionless. Like they were caught in the headlights on foot on some congested highway. If they go right, they are dead. If they go left, they are dead. They must balance on the centerline.

I obviously did something to fall off the center.

The others will be careful not to say something, anything that will call his attention away from me and onto them.

Where are those angels? Oh, they are telling me I'm in danger—

to rise up, stand up, tell the big people that ***this meeting is over****!*

I feel some kind of blackness or evil surrounding me, chill bumps running down my legs. Maybe I'm evil. The radio preacher thinks we are all evil.

Women executives do not cry, Donna. You're like the CEO of a big company. You can't cry. Hold back the tears.

The strawheads looked sharply to one side and then the other, hoping their heads didn't get blown up, leaving shreds of straw all over the floor.

The tears are here. I feel my wet cheeks. "Mrs. Orchard you will draft a letter to Senator Flagstaff and tell her that her daughter cannot attend your school this year."

"Mr. Matson must have made a deal with her to let her child in Davenport without going through the selection process," I said. " Her name just showed up on the role. Senator Flagstaff came in this summer, but I don't know what they talked about. I have not placed anyone on the roll who was not sent to me from the Magnet Office."

"Mrs. Orchard, get that letter off today. School opens in two weeks. Tell her that a mistake has been made. I want you to do your job, Mrs. Orchard. That student should have never enrolled in your school."

"Yes, Sir. But Senator Flagstaff has probably already bought the uniforms for Davenport."

I can't defend myself. The superintendent, the Ph.D.s, the Senator. I never wanted to fight. It was my daddy who liked to fight. I am just little Don trying to survive here with all the big people in this cold cage. When will you let me out? They wanted to bring me to tears, even the strawhead women, no tears. All dry faces. They smelled blood. They will follow the angry man with fine, thin lips, red hair and a red face. They will go home to their strawhead families tonight, "A good day? Yes, it was a good day."

"Mrs. Orchard, did you hear me?"

"Yes, Dr. Barker, I'll draft the letter today."

The strawheads rolled their button eyes to the ceiling.

Popping popcorn at basketball games, washing cars, driving vans to cheerleader camp, taking students home at ten at night, all for this. Congratulations, Donna. You have arrived! I just got my last degree when I was fifty years old and still have student loans. The superintendent never intends to keep me.

When I got up to leave, I looked down to see straw piled under my chair. Of course, I was a placater, too. I could be as disingenuous as anyone around the table. I would never have made it to middle management if I had not played the game. If my head was not being offered up for sacrifice today, I could be one of the bloodthirsty feral cats. Yes. I would be one of the silent henchmen so as not to make a wrong move, only to find my own head under the chair.

Chapter 15

DID I MENTION THIS?

Did I mention that everything is about race in public schools in the South? I think of what my retired principal friend, Jack, said when I became an administrator. "You may love your inner city kids and they may even love you, but when it comes right down to it," he looked down and rubbed my arm, "you'll never be one of them. Donna, welcome to a place where you are sure to get your heart broken."

Mobile's population is fifty-five percent African-American and forty-five percent Caucasian. There is a constant push/pull, a deep-seated suspicion in both camps. Decisions should be made within the practical considerations of race. However, race had become the starting point, or at best, a smoke screen for every decision made, from the school board to the city council.

I considered Davenport Magnet a beautiful exception to these holdovers from an old Gulf Coast City. The students played music together, danced together, sang together and painted colorful murals on decaying downtown buildings—together.

I read recently about a school, The Hand In Hand School in Jerusalem—one of five such—opened in 1998. It is a bilingual academy whose students are nearly fifty percent Jewish and fifty percent Arab. The principal, Nadia Kinani, an Arab said, "We are all here. We have to figure out a way to live together."

The students at Davenport Magnet had figured out how to live together.

The adults had not.

When I walked into the school on my first day as principal, one of my friends pulled me aside, "I heard they are not going to keep you. Cedric Lane has been told he will replace you at the end of the year." He was African American.

The committee started meeting in my brain, the confusion. When the Birdie Mae Davis desegregation case was ended one year before, one of the requirements to stay out of Federal Court was for the system to hire more African American principals. The law suit had cost the system millions of dollars and no one wanted to go back to those days. I was not so naïve as to believe that the minority school board members would 'give up' the principalship of the magnet school charitably.

Neither was I a part of the superintendent's group of trusted colleagues.

Some aspects of being a principal came naturally to me. The creativity between the talented staff of teachers and I played off each other and some good ideas were born.

After visiting the art room for the last three years, I looked to my left at a black curtain and realized that we were not utilizing the dark room for photography. I met two women photographers at art openings in Mobile and knew something about their work. A plan surfaced; they began to volunteer their time to teach a photography class once a week after school. A collection of professional cameras was there for the students' use. With these traditional cameras, art and math wed, as students acquired expertise in adjusting settings manually for light, distance, and focus. Lining the halls were original black and white photographs of lighthouses, puppies, homeless street people, moon pies: photographs by the students and developed at the school.

Everything should be running smoothly. Right?

Wrong.

I received a letter the day before school opened from Senator Virginia Flagstaff. She was responding to my letter ordered by the superintendent that informed her, "I'm sorry. You're daughter cannot attend Davenport Magnet School this year."

Senator Virginia Flagstaff
(D)
Senate Majority Leader
Room 7726
11 South Union Street
Montgomery, Alabama 36130

Donna F. Orchard, Principal
Davenport Magnet School for the Performing Arts
11 South Warren Street
Mobile, AL 36701
September 6, 1999

Dear Ms. Orchard:

I stepped into my house from a buying trip with my daughter to get her school uniforms when I saw your letter lying on the breakfast table.

I called the school on August 12 to be sure Jasmine was on roll at Davenport. The registrar found her name on the enrollment list.

You can imagine my surprise to receive your letter informing me that my daughter cannot attend Davenport this year because her name was not chosen in the lottery system this summer.

I talked to Mr. Matson in July before he left and he assured me that my daughter could attend your school, the middle school closest to our home. She will be living with her grandmother while I am in Montgomery during the legislative sessions.

The Flagstaff law firm advised me that an oral contract was made in July and verified in writing by the registrar in August.

I am sure that this matter can be cleared up with the superintendent in a timely fashion and we can then work together in Jasmine's best interest.

Sincerely,

Virginia Florence Flagstaff

Virginia Florence Flagstaff

cc: Dr. Thomas Barker, Superintendent

Two weeks after school opened, the superintendent's secretary called and told me to add a name to my enrollment: Jasmine Flagstaff.

Knowing the faculty could only be a plus. They understood my direct style.

Our relationship; however, was now vastly different. Teachers who were my friends suddenly became solicitous. It seemed that everyone wanted something from me.

A little fourth grade girl ran into my office during third period one day. "A big middle school boy pushed me into the boy's restroom when I was upstairs going to jazz class! He's been doing that to the girls every day!"

I was sensitive to the fact that there were two schools: an elementary school with grades 4th and 5th in one building and a middle school, grades 6-8, in the other. It was important for the younger children to feel safe when they came into the middle school for classes. This led to an impetuous decision on my part, clearly unfair to the

African American student— a ten-day suspension for what turned out to be a minor offense. There was nothing sexual involved in the restroom incident. The middle school boy was just being silly. A call to his father put him back in school; however, the father was a prominent pastor in the community. Once the rumor that I was a racist was dropped upstream, it went gushing down the rocks as fact.

Leadership is often about perception. I was under a new covenant. The principal at Davenport who hired me as his assistant stayed at school until five o'clock every day chatting with people while slowly opening one envelope after another in the mailbag.

I was not aware this first year that the informal time with faculty and staff could be used to work through problems and resolve misunderstandings. I felt depleted at the end of the day and was not patient about hanging around after the students were gone. The perception: The principal is not here—enough.

I heard through gossip that the superintendent's impending plan was to call me in and fire me before the end of the year. Dire consequences. I needed legal advice. The menacing had progressed to a new level. My ability to make a living was being jeopardized. *I need somebody on my side.*

My lawyer liked me and said he would write a letter to the superintendent. I do not remember what he wrote, probably something like: *Lay off my client you egg sucker. She's been in this field for almost twenty-five years, you nitwit*—but in lawyer speak.

Do not have a lawyer write a letter to your boss until you are on your way out the door. I had not completed my three years' probation as a principal. The tenure law was on the side of the superintendent.

In good standing with the teacher's union, I went to them for help. "You can be fired without cause if you are not tenured at the principal level."

The last rational course of action—before I got to the Africatown Bridge solution—was to find a psychiatrist. Therapy might help me with the decision, fight or flight.

The tall handsome psychiatrist had me lie down on a table, then turn over. Later he suggested that we sit down on the rug and do exercises together, breathe and become centered, get our bodies in touch with the universe. Not the right psychiatrist. I figured out quickly what his hands on therapy meant and used the restroom getaway.

The next psychiatrist was a polite Asian man who spoke English with difficulty. I started jabbering nonsense, my default with strangers—especially a psychiatrist—until I am comfortable. He sat quietly and listened, staring at me with a big question mark in his eyes.

Then he began. "Mis-ses Or-chard, please begin counting from one hundred to one by sevens."

"Huh?" *Oh, I got it. He wants to find out if I'm insane. I'll play along with him and his wacko game.* "Now what do you want me to do?"

"Count backward from one hundred to one by sevens." His expression never changed.

"Okay. Backward by sevens. Ninety-three. *Umm. I didn't know I'd have to do math. Just needed to talk to somebody…Shit, I am crazy!* I got up. "I've got to go." The restroom getaway again.

I ran to the car and leaned over the steering wheel. *I didn't want to ask if I could use my fingers for the math.*

When I went to a final meeting with Dr. Barker, I asked him, "Why are you so angry? You don't know me. I've never had a conversation with you."

"I'm not angry! You'll know it when I get angry!" he said.

Mr. Monroe, the closest thing I had to a mentor, was at the meeting. He asked Dr. Barker if a principalship to another school was possible for me.

Dr. Barker said, "no."

There was still an idea in the South that women did not really have to work; we had husbands to take care of us.

I remember standing out by the curb at Parker years before, watching an ambulance drive away as the EMTs went to work with needles, bags and beeping machines on the student who had been stabbed in the gut at recess. I walked slowly back into my office, my whole body still shaking.

A few minutes later, a parent arrived for an appointment. She came into my office and asked, "How are you, Mrs. Orchard?"

"Umm. Fine. How are you? What can I do for you today?"

School counselors are set up to talk with children after a traumatic incident. In contrast, administrators often cannot readily share feelings to decompress and stabilize their equilibrium. I had long-term health effects from denying my physical and emotional limitations.

A favorite novel, *A Separate Peace*, by John Knowles, has come back to haunt me over the years. Gene and Finny were college friends. Finny was a superior athlete and Gene excelled in academics. What began one weekend as college hijinks between the two friends, turned tragic. There was a branch over the river that they had swung off many times, diving out into the deep water.

That day, Gene shook the branch, just as Finny jumped; he fell short causing a permanent injury. Athletic competition for him was over. The reader was engaged in the question: Was it an accident? Or because of jealousy, did Gene shake the branch intentionally, causing harm to his friend?

I'm not sure why it was the Africatown Bridge as opposed to the Dolly Parton Bridge or any other bridge that I imagined as my way out of my feelings of humiliation. Maybe it was because when my African American support was lost, I knew everything was lost.

Because of my boys, my grandchildren and all my schoolchildren, I slowly worked through Elizabeth Kubler-Ross's four stages of grief to acceptance. It became clear: It did not matter if I was pushed or if I unwittingly found myself in the wrong place at the wrong time—my career was over. An energetic fifty-four, I could die of self-pity or I could take stock and decide who I was if I wasn't a principal.

One of those spiritual moments happened on a downtown street when my artist friend, Fred Marchman, grabbed my arm on the sidewalk and said, "Let's go into this estate auction."

In the first of several rooms, I eyed a piece of folk art that I adored, but I had to wait for three hours for it to come up for bids. The angel, a halo over a small face, tiny wings behind, wore a long red skirt with small white polka dots that covered the entire vertical canvas down to little feet peeking out at the bottom. It was hand-painted on a long narrow shutter salvaged from a New Orleans shotgun style cottage. I had $200 in my pocket that did *not* represent a discretionary line item in my budget for 'artwork' that month.

I raised my card and started the biding, "$100.00."

A voice from behind me,"$125."

The auctioneer looked at me and queried, "$150?"

I took a chance, "$135."

Silence… "And it's yours for one hundred and thirty-five dollars," he banged his gavel and pointed to me!

The tall angel over the fireplace vaults my eye to the twelve-foot ceiling when I sit in the living room in my comfortable red chair, a tartan over my legs. I think of my Al-Anon friend, Joe, who told me to take my angels with me when I'm scared little Donna. He is up among the stars now. "Hey Joe, my angels are with me."

But when an undertaking occasionally did fail, I was filled with resentment and depression that could be cured only by the next triumph. Very early, therefore, I came to value everything in terms of victory or defeat— "all or nothing." The only satisfaction I knew was to win.

Only through utter defeat are we able to take our first steps toward liberation and strength. Our admissions of personal powerlessness finally turn out to be a firm bedrock upon which happy and purposeful lives may be built.

As Bill Sees It: The A.A. Way of Life (selected writings of A.A.'s co-founder)

After being demoted back to an assistant principal, I worked in a high school for one year before I was eligible for retirement. I was no longer willing to work for the school system in Mobile. The untenable situation meant that I would never again make a living even close to the \$60,000 I made as a principal.

I needed to heal physically and emotionally. I am in debt to the small private school where I worked for the next six years. Developing a deep respect and affection for the director of the school and the faculty, I got back to my first love—teaching.

Bill and I were able to keep our cottage and remain in the area close to friends and family.

Donna (left) and Marilyn

Chapter 16

RAW FAITH: THE FILM

I called my sister recently and we had the same memoir in our hands—soul sisters.

We have a special bond for lots of reasons, but I figure that being born on the same day is as good as it gets. Oh, we are different. I am the workhorse type, on the fringes, in the trenches. Marilyn lives in Portland, Oregon, in the Northwest, above the fray, analyzing all the big and little frays for the rest of us.

When we travel together, I carry her bags into the motel, tell her what time to get up, and remind her that we had better go or we'll be late.

I depend on her to kick me out of my comfort zone and make me aware of my, too large, footprint in the environment. She reminds me not to eat things that might kill me, or worse, make me fat which would then…add to my footprint.

"Donna go on line and read my blog if you want to know what's on my mind."

"Think I'll just call you up, Sis."

"Donna, you don't shop at that Big Box store! You don't, do you? They don't pay for their employees' health insurance. Don't you have a Trader Joe's down there?"

"No, I only see them here. By the way, I told a cab driver yesterday when I flew into Portland that I was from Alabama and he asked, 'Why would anybody live down there?'"

Marilyn pulled into Trader's to shop for organic stuff for dinner. It was already eight o'clock before my sister thought about eating.

She handed me a dozen brown eggs for the buggy. "Donna, you have to buy eggs from free roaming, nesting hens—cage free chickens, fed with natural grains."

"I guess we have those on the Gulf Coast. Can they roam in sand?"

"Oh, Donna. Anyway, do you know how most of the chickens are bred today? Thousands are grown in total darkness because they fatten up faster that way. Stuffed into huge chicken warehouses with no room to move, they dawdle in their own feces. When their bodies get fat quicker than their frames, they flop around and fall down on their little spindly legs and suffocate each other before they are slaughtered."

"That sounds horrible. I can't stand to think about it."

"Well, we better think about it. In recent years, just a few companies have taken control of our whole food supply. Three or four companies supply all the pork, the beef, and process all the chickens. This has all happened in the last few years; all the big companies have swallowed up the smaller ones. And the beef, look over here, Donna. You can get beef from cows that graze on grass in a field, all natural beef. No antibiotics. No growth hormones. Humanely treated."

"I see cows in the fields every morning on my way to work. They look pretty happy."

"That's just a few head of cattle the farmers grow for their own use. You get most of your meat from the big companies. Have you heard the names Tindale, Hebson? That's where you get your meat. Young girls are maturing much too soon because they get all of these hormones in the meat they eat, and in the milk."

"Yeah, you know I've noticed that, Sis, as I've worked with children over the years. Girls are reaching puberty earlier and earlier, some at eleven and twelve."

"It's the hormones fed to the beef cattle. Cows should graze lackadaisical, naturally on grass. They should not be packed together so tightly they can't move and made to feed on grain all day, then stand in their own feces."

"Sis, could we stop talking about poo until after we've eaten dinner?"

When I was on the plane traveling to Portland, I felt satisfied about my life.

On the flight home, I began to stress over finding a side of beef from a natural farm. *Who will want to share it with me? I can start with the eggs. The eggs will be easy. Why am I such a sluggard who sits by and lets the world go to hell?*

People in Del City, the little town in North Louisiana where we grew up, had high expectations of my older sister. She exceeded all of them: all 'As' in high school, summa cum laude from Louisiana Tech, Fulbright Scholar to the University of Arkansas for graduate school and a Ph.D. in theology and the arts from Berkeley.

Having become a minister and luminary among the intelligentsia in the Northwest, Marilyn called me down South to say, "Donna there's going to be a documentary made about me next year. I will be filmed for a whole year, maybe two. My family will be interviewed. Will you do it? We might even take it to Sundance. It'll be fun. What about it?"

"Oh, what is it about?"

"The movie? Well, it's about me. Two filmmakers in my congregation thought that my ideas, my politics, should have national exposure. They encouraged me to see if I could find funding for the project. I talked to a friend who is doing well in stocks up in Seattle. She liked the idea and gave me some money to get started. We've already hired a professional filmmaker."

"Well, what is it going to be about?"

"Donna, I told you...ugh, it is going to be about my ideas, my social justice work. But after he started looking at the project, Peter thinks it should be a more personal film, the through line will be my transition from the ministry when I retire next year, where I'll go; what I'll do. It will be a huge change for me, Donna. My work in the ministry has been my life for the last seventeen years."

"It's been that long?"

"Yeah. And I can't even attend my former church where all of my friends are, at least not for a couple of years, until the new minister takes hold."

"What do they want me to do, gaze into your eyes while you give me wise counsel? Just kidding, Sis. I'll try to get the Oscar for 'Best Supporting Actor in a female role.' I've had plenty of practice. Okay, I'll stop with the jokes."

"No, really. It's going to be a ninety-minute film, a full-length movie. They'll want to sit down and talk with you at some point"

"Sure, Marilyn, it sounds like fun. How much ya gonna pay me?"

"Oh, Donna."

When we got to Del City for a week with the film crew, Peter, the director and Trevor, the cameraman, it was easy to see how we all rapidly became new best friends. Peter pulled on my bra strap and lifted the waist of my jeans to thread me down and hook me up, then had to do it all again, until every word was clear.

Marilyn and I treated the guys to fried catfish and boiled crawfish on the lake, sang our old hymns and laughed, cried some; and we all did become very close for a time as we showed Peter and Trevor the South.

Headlong, we began interacting with the film as an entity with its own personality, much like a baby takes hold of a family the day Mama comes home with the news. There were Marilyn (the sister), Marilyn (the 'talent'), Peter, Trevor and me, four strangers trekking around Del City, companions of 'the film.'

Suddenly, life became exciting, quickened, movable; if one shot didn't work, take another. *I think I like this.*

Peter, the diplomatic corps of one, said several times, "Donna, we can hear you fine, just speak normally." He did not know I got my normal voice training in a high school gym—where I could break up a fight down on the other end by yelling, "Fellows… if I have to walk down there…." Finally Peter said, "Here, Donna, put on these head phones and see what you sound like." *It's too late for me Peter. Don't you understand? You got me too late.*

When Marilyn and I approached Del City in my liberal Passat wagon with 'Hillary for President' on the bumper (not knowing it would have to last until 2016), we were bobbing our heads, singing our oldies. We forgot we were hooked up for audio or we didn't care.

As we rounded the curve across from the railroad track, "Look, Donna, the name of that business is 'Lightening Garage.' Must be fifty cars crowded out front. Think they should change the name?" Then we howled with laughter like sisters do, knowing the story would get better with the telling. Meanwhile Peter and Trevor who were squatting in a van behind us shooting, tapped their feet…waited. I could tell they did not think it was *that* funny.

"Don't put on the brakes, Donna. Trevor is shooting."

"Well, what if I have to?"

"Trevor will fall out!"

"That will sure change the plot."

"Oh, Donna."

"There's where the Ho-Maid used to be, I remembered. It's a tire store now. One time you and I had burgers and fries there when you came home from college. When we pulled away, I threw my sack and all my trash out the window and you told me to never do that. You said that we would be covered up in garbage if everybody did that. I never littered again."

All the little shanties were sitting on the hills heading into town, exposing the poverty of the little town, exactly where they were fifty years before. We remembered 'Colored' water fountains and restrooms and when blacks had to sit in the balcony in the movie theater. That was what we knew. It was shocking to Marilyn and me now that this warped treatment was commonplace to us.

"There's no place to work in Del City, Donna. The young people moved out to larger cities," Marilyn reminded me.

When the school board 'integrated' the schools one year after I graduated, in 1966, the white high school became almost totally black and the white community opened a private school between Del City and Carlton, a town about seventeen miles away. It is one of the few public school systems still segregated. Having worked in public schools most of my life now, I am confounded that my own high school was never successfully integrated.

I knew from years of teaching in inner city public schools that the display of the Confederate flag terrorized many black students and adults. A conspicuous Southern symbol, this image on the back windows of pickup trucks and even in some restaurants is a message to *keep out,* and the not-so-subtle warning, *it could mean much more.*

When we rode by the private school on the edge of town, we saw that the entire front of the long red brick building was draped with a giant Confederate flag, no door visible from the street. Frightened at the sight, my legs started shaking, then nausea. Why would a menacing display be exhibited on a school building? What a heavy, arduous task it must have been! How could a flag that large even be made? What determination to strike fear into the heart of the observer!

After I fully internalized what happened, the tears came with an overwhelming sadness and disappointment. The segregated school system remains a deep loss for this small town. The population remains a stagnant 5000. Many of the stores I remembered on the main square are closed and the one Wal-Mart on the edge of town is closed. Our visitors surely stepped back in time.

Confederate States of America

I had a memory about the time I was coaching tennis in an urban high school in Mobile in the 80s. I was driving my tennis team in the school van to a residential white community bordering theirs for a match.

"We don't go across that line, over into that town." Cedric said.

I looked at him confused, "What do you mean? You know we have a match."

"I'm not going," Lateesha spoke up as she slid down onto the floorboard.

Then Fredrick dove down with her. "I'm not going over there either."

"Listen, you can go anywhere you want to! This is a free country! You're with me and we are going over here to play tennis."

Anger. Disappointment, sadness, confusion, fear; all of my emotions flip right over to anger. *I've got to work on that.*

"Okay, Mrs. Orchard, don't get so upset." They looked at each other... I guess we'll go."

Marilyn shivered, "That huge flag gives me the creeps, covering the whole front entrance to the school."

"Let's tell the guys we want to stop for coffee." I felt embarrassed.

"Donna, you mean pie and coffee."

"So."

"Ma'am," Peter spoke to our server, "We wondered if we could bring our camera in and film while we are in here. We are making a movie about this woman who grew up in Del City." He pointed to Marilyn and she smiled sweetly. "Is that okay?"

She gave him a disembodied look, "I just work here. I'm your waitress. I'll go ask the manager...He said, 'I reckon so', but I don't want no pictures of me. I'll just get your order and give you the ticket. Then I won't be back over to this table."

"Of course not. Sure. Thanks."

She was agitated. I could tell she felt vulnerable.

I understood skittishness around a camera. While I was waiting for Marilyn and the guys to finish filming in the restaurant, I thought of another camera that had struck fear in my own heart. I was in New Orleans in 2009 with Grace, a friend of mine doing research for a book on the local cuisine. Through some people she knew, we were able to connect with a woman in New Orleans whose family went back five generations. She agreed to meet with us and help us with logistics when we got to the city.

We left Fairhope and traveled to St. Charles Street in New Orleans to find the towering white antebellum home. We parked under the big oaks and looked up to see an intimate porch with black grillwork off each of the top two stories.

When our host heard about the project she said, "You should go to one of my favorite restaurants, but" she whispered, "you can't go alone. I'll have to go with you... to make the introductions... and let the owner know you are with me."

We looked at each other for a minute... and said, "We'd like to walk around to see your garden and talk about our schedule for the day."

When we got outside, "She means the Mafia owns the restaurant," Grace explained.

"No!" I gasped.

"She said that she would have to go with us, Donna."

We continued to discuss the veiled invitation strolling in her manicured tropical courtyard amid large cascading jelly palms, gigantic spit-leaf philodendron and thorny pyracantha bushes with red berries scaling the brick wall.

We decided to accompany her to the mysterious restaurant, to be risk takers, for the sake of our art.

When driving there our host said, "Walk behind me through the door and don't say a word. I'll introduce you and tell 'the man' you are with me."

"Which man?" I asked.

She looked at me a little surprised, "You'll know."

When we walked into the dark interior and headed toward the back, each person at the long bar to our right turned around slightly, heads ducked to glance at us.

A man in a white shirt—three buttons opened at the top—and gray dress pants moved out of the shadows and headed in our direction. He was loose and easygoing, however; he said 'hello,' with a faux warmth that was unemotional and impersonal, as though we had walked into a family gathering uninvited.

Before we finished the turtle soup and got our entrée of crawfish etouffee, 'the man' walked over to our table with a camera, a large, outdated model I had not seen in years. Without saying a word, he focused on our faces to get a close-up, then in a few seconds, the camera spit out a hard copy. We watched him tear it off and put it in his shirt pocket.

The committee for Marilyn's Fiftieth Del City High School Class Reunion which was held that weekend, decided not to let Peter film it. A few of Marilyn's friends agreed to an interview elsewhere.

"I'm not sure I can find Daddy's grave, Marilyn. Jimmy and I were here last year and we went up and down the rows in this cemetery and we couldn't find it."

Marilyn looked around. "It's right by Granny and Big Papa."

"I know, but we couldn't find any of them."

Marilyn insisted, "We'll find it. Peter might want to use it in the film."

"Here's a Fulmer gravestone, but that is Uncle Ezzie's family. There's Lavel right next to Uncle Ezzie. Uncle Ezzie used to take me to singin's on Sunday afternoon in the Studebaker that didn't have a back seat. Alexis Reed and I would dress alike and sing *The Solid Rock.*" Marilyn and I broke into song, "On Christ the solid rock I stand, all other ground is sinking sand, all other ground is.... sin...king... sand."

"Take the high part, Donna."

"Oh, I forgot. Let's try it again..."

Marilyn cried when we could not find our daddy.

The next day we turned onto Fulmer Street— named after our grandfather who had been postmaster. I knew every crack and crevice on that street.

I began the tour for Peter. "On the left is Miss Kinebrew's big house with a grassy field up that terrace where we played touch football. Next is the Lay's old two story that used to be nice. Diane was my age and—mean."

Marilyn thought about her coach. "Then the coach moved into the Lay's house. They had a bunch of kids. Do you remember that, Donna? He had the affair with the art teacher who was married to Diddly Porter, one of the meanest men in Del City. Coach Gibson came to class to tell us goodbye and he had a black eye!"

Next was Miss Lennie Craigler's house surrounded by grassy terraces on all sides, two magnolia trees in the front yard. "She was the only widow-woman on the street. When her husband Fred, the bank president, failed to come home one night, Miss Lennie called the police. They found him in the bank vault with a bullet in his head, the gun by his side. Remember, Marilyn? You would go to spend the night with Miss Lennie to keep her company. After the tragedy, right up until her death, she was known on Fulmer Street as the widow-woman. Years later, someone was sure to bring up her name when the ladies rocked on our front porch shelling purple hill peas. As if they still couldn't believe it, they'd recollect the night that Fred got a gun and blew his brains out, right up there at the bank, then shake their heads in unison humming, my, my, my."

Next was Miss Lee's house, the old maid. I considered that even weirder than being a widow woman.

Our house at 609 Fulmer stood at the foot of the street for all to see, just like my grandfather who took his place at the head of the table at every meal.

I was surprised that our old home place seemed so much bigger in my child's eye. It looked compressed to me now, to almost dollhouse size. The house was a colonial style with a porch, half hidden by nandina bushes, running the length of the house, and two white columns framing the front door. What I remembered out front as a huge oak tree was small in comparison to the regal oaks in Mobile.

This yard and house, my launching pad into the world, seemed vast to me then because of the entanglements of childhood.

Marilyn insisted on knocking on the door to ask the current owner if we could come in and film.

"I'm going to stay in the car," I said.

When a cordial black man came to the door, he said that we could set up a time to come back the next day.

Anticlimactic for me, I did not recognize anything when we went into our family home the next day. The rooms had been reconfigured and walls moved. I did see the long built-in window seat that ran the length of the dining room, our bedroom, after Marilyn and I moved in with our grandparents.

It was no longer home.

We have now announced that such segregation is a denial of the equal protection of the laws. In order that we may have the full assistance of the parties, the cases will be restored to the docket for further argument on specified questions relating to the forms of the decrees.

Brown vs. Board of Education of Topeka

Chapter 17

THE SWIMMING POOL

In 2011, I picked up the *Mobile Press-Register* from the breakfast room table, 'Seven Teens Die in Red River on the 4th.' *Red River is close to Shreveport and a familiar name from my childhood. How could seven teenagers die in a river? Did their boat overturn?*

I read on. The day before, at a Fourth of July picnic with his family, one of the teens went out too far in the river, got into trouble and called for help. His buddies, who couldn't swim either, went out to try to save him. All seven of the healthy young teens died.

The newspaper reported that the parents watched helplessly from the bank, yelling for someone, anyone, because none of them could swim.

At the public swimming pool in Del City, there was no sign, *No Coloreds.* A lawyer would say it was defacto, by custom, just a fact of life, and it was.

Among the familiar places I wanted to see during the filming visit was the public swimming pool that animated my long summer days. By fall, my blond hair was a pile of green cotton candy from the chorine. I wanted to see the blue water I remembered and the high board where daddy thrilled us with his dives.

The distance across town did not seem as far as it did years ago when I peddled my bike around the corner by the Tatum's big house, then up the hill to the divided road leading to the pool, about a mile.

As I approached and parked in the summer sun, I began to wonder… *I wonder… Where are all the cars and screams from the children in the baby pool?* I rushed toward the side, looked through the chain link fence and stopped short. Stunned. Horrified. The Olympic-sized pool that was the lively center of our play, was now a huge dry hole scattered with black leaves and brown branches. My tears could have filled it up.

I was suddenly overcome by a macabre image—of children, stomachs flat in this dry hole trying to flip over, like a bass from a cool river thrown into a dry bucket.

The intermittent spots of blue paint from the bottom were enough to give rise in me a nagging hope that this pool could be reclaimed for duty someday. *What had happened?*

I learned that the pool that held so many of my childhood memories was closed when black children showed up to swim, challenging segregation in the 60s in the light of the 1954 ruling *Brown v the Board of Education* and the 1964 Civil Rights Act. No child, black or white, has learned to swim in the pool for nearly fifty years. The public swimming pool remains a gaping wound in the psyche of this small town.

~

I visited the Del City High School where we went to school. Walking past the tall columns and into the grand front entrance of the classical red brick building were large group pictures of each graduating class lining the walls to the top of the high ceilings. Beginning with the most recent, I was obsessed with finding my 1965 class, the last one before desegregation, forty white faces

In 1966, there was a shockingly small graduating class—all African American. As I walked down the rows to the present day, I found that there are still only four or five white students with each graduating class of about fifty—not a true representation of the population of the small town.

Afterword

VICTOR

Years after I morphed from educator to writer, I was heading to visit my four grandchildren in Mobile when a tire blew out. You don't want to have a blowout on crowded Airport Boulevard in Mobile at rush hour. I whipped my wheel around into the nearest garage.

Jumping out in frustration, I could see the tire was a mess.

"Hello, Ma'am, what can I do for you?"

That's a familiar voice. I unwrapped myself from around the sick tire and looked up, "Oh. Hi. You look familiar to me. Did I teach you?"

"You were my principal."

"Did I beat you? Just kidding. Don't tell me your name. Give me a minute… Is it Victor?"

"Yes? You have to remember me, Ms. O. I was your favorite student."

"It's a relief to see your face, Victor. As you can see I've had a blowout."

"Let me look." He rubbed his finger along the tread and stopped at the wide gash. This cut is at an angle. I can't repair that unfortunately. You'll have to get a new tire. What do you want to do? Do you have a spare?..."

When I was all fixed up and ready to go, "Well, Victor is this a good job for you?" I was curious.

"Okay. It's a good part-time job, but I don't get medical. I'm in school at Bishop State. I'm going to be a teacher. I'll bet you can't believe that! My grades weren't so good in middle school."

"Great. Victor. What good news! I **can** believe it. You were the captain of the peer mediation team at Parker. Do you remember?"

"Yeah. I remember that we could get out of class."

"Oh, Victor... Just remember. The first year of teaching, well, uh... is the hardest. Go through that door, hunker down, and get through that first year. Everything I could have done wrong, I did wrong, that first year. I cried a lot. It does get better. I promise you. I'm one of those lucky people who likes kids. If you like children, Victor—if they give you energy—stick with teaching. I know you'll do well. There's nothing like seeing one of you grow up, set some goals and take that next step in life. How is your buddy, Tremaine, from middle school...?"

The Idea of Education

All I say is, call things by their right names, and do not confuse together ideas which are essentially different. A thorough knowledge of one science and a superficial acquaintance with many are not the same thing; a smattering of a hundred things or a memory for detail, is not a...comprehensive view...Do not say, the people must be educated, when, after all you only mean amused, refreshed, soothed, put into good spirits and good humor, or kept from vicious excesses...Education is a high word; it is the preparation for knowledge, and it is the imparting of knowledge in proportion to that preparation...It is education which gives a man a clear conscious view of his own opinions and judgments, a truth in developing them, an eloquence in expressing them, and a force in urging them. It teaches him to see things as they are, to go right to the point, to disentangle a skein of thought, to detect what is sophistical, and to discard what is irrelevant. It shows him how to accommodate himself to others, how to throw himself into their state of mind, how to bring before them his own, how to influence them, how to come to an understanding with them, how to bear with them...He knows when to speak and when to be silent; he is able to converse, he is able to listen; he can ask a question pertinently, and gain a lesson seasonable, when nothing to impart himself.

JOHN HENRY NEWMAN (1851)

Discourses on the Scope and Nature of a University Education, which in 1952 became *The Idea of a University*

References

Carmichael, S. and Hamilton C.V. (1967). *The Politics of Liberation in America*. New York. Random House.

Chandler, D. (2002). *Semiotics for Beginners.* London. Taylor and Frances Group.

Klein, J. (December 15, 2014). *Time.* vol.184, no. 23. New York. Time, Inc.

Knowles, J. (1959). *A Separate Peace*. London. Secker and Warburg.

Kubler-Ross, E.. (1969*). On Death and Dying.* New York City. Scribner.

Patterson, J.T. (2001*). Brown v. Board of Education: A Civil Rights Milestone and Its Troubled Legacy.* Oxford. Oxford University Press.

Rawn, J. Jr. (2010). *Root and Branch: Charles Hamilton Houston, Thurgood Marshall, and the Struggle to End Segregation.* New York. Bloomsbury Press.

Summitt, P. with Sally Jenkins (1999). reprint *Reach for the Summit.* New York. Crown Publishing Group.

Tushnet, M.V. Editor. (2001). *Thurgood Marshall: His Speeches, Writings, Arguments, Opinions, and Reminiscences.* Chicago. Lawrence Hill Books.

Williams, J. (1998). *Thurgood Marshall: American Revolutionary*. New York. Three Rivers Press.

Wilson, B. (1967) *As Bill Sees It: The A.A. Way of Life (selected writings of A.A.'s co- founder).* New York. Alcoholics Anonymous World Services, Inc.

WE SHOULDN'T LET OUR SCHOOLS RESEGREGATE

In 1969, when I had just turned 22, I walked into my first teaching job at a high school in north Louisiana. Federal marshals walked in right behind me. They were there to enforce the 1954 *Brown v. Board of Education ruling*. Separate would no longer be considered equal.

Retired from the public system in Mobile, I am sad that the resegregation of K-12 schools seems to be taking root. There are some exceptions, including our K-8 magnet schools and Murphy High School, which has always had a naturally diverse student body.

However, it concerns me that many of the initiatives in the 1970s, 1980s and 1990s were simply dropped with the end of the Birdie Mae Davis desegregation case, with nothing to take their place.

Each year, schools are increasingly homogeneous.

We have a global economy and a more diverse populace than ever before. We all have a stake in having an educated community.

Our students will not be prepared for such a world if we go back to the old ways.

DONNA F. ORCHARD
Robertsdale

About the Author

DONNA F. ORCHARD

donnaforchard@gmail.com

Donna Orchard is an advocate for children. She has worked as a teacher and administrator in public middle schools and high schools in the South. Her work has included teaching in county facilities and juvenile halls.

She is a writer working out of her home office in Robertsdale, Alabama.